By

Lisa Vandepol

Publisher

Lisa Vandepol

Toronto, ON

Canada

Printed in Canada and the United States of America

The New Bucket List

www.thenewbucketlist.com

ACKNOWLEDGEMENTS

This was not an easy book to write. Who knew you had to do so much research?? It's like English class all over again! That being said, I have people to thank for inspiring me, guiding me and supporting me through this whole process. I would never have completed this book without you coming into my life.

TL;DR Thank you! You're amazing! You have inspired me to finish my first book!

Raymond Aaron – Waaaay back, my dad took me to a seminar that introduced me to the notion of writing a book. It had never EVER occurred to me as it seemed like you had to be 'special' to do it. You taught me that anyone could write a book and created the program that can make it all happen...did I follow it? Not totally, but I did use your framework to get the ball rolling. This book would have never happened if I hadn't enrolled in your program.

Dad. So, this is truly all your fault. You brought me to see Raymond Aaron and the seed was planted. The discussions we have about life, challenges, risks, success and failure are talks I will always cherish. You always believed in me. Always. It didn't matter what I said I was going to do, you encouraged me to do it. I cannot thank you enough for the support from someone I love. Love you!

To my mom, and my super awesome stepdad AKA Brian and Nan. The first time I mentioned writing a book, you all shrugged it off, like "I'll believe it when I see it." Even though I was discouraged, I still knew I would write a book one day. It took almost 10 years to find something I was passionate enough to write a book about, but here it is. Told you I'd write a book! HA!

Natalie Gomes of Cooking Quidnunc – Oh, Nat. You must know that this book is kind of your fault. I would whine that Instagram was annoying and that I would delete it all in a second, when you'd say, "Well, you've gotta work on what's important to you." You were absolutely right. Writing was always important to me and here we are! Thank you so much for being an amazing friend and travel buddy. I'm truly grateful to have you in my life!

Tiffany and Craig of BAOS Podcast – Thank you for inspiring me. You embodied my favourite quote from Tom Bilyeu, "Will you get so good that you become the excuse that other people use not to try?" You're killing it! I didn't try to wiggle my way in where I felt there was no space for me, but you were also the reason I tried, and I succeeded at making space for myself using what I'm passionate about. Don't stop being awesome.

Mike Pickett - The Hero Mission – When you asked if anyone wanted to speak at your first event, I knew I had to do it…even though I couldn't look at the keyboard as I typed YES. I wasn't ready to do my first public speaking gig, but somehow, you knew I'd be fine. Your huge heart and relentless encouragement made it a day I will never forget. Thank you for believing in me.

The Inner Circle with Lewis Howes – When I struggled finding like-minded people, I found this group. Gary Henderson, Bradley Will, Melanie McMurrain, Lewis Howes and all of the incredible members kept me going. Having this group there to answer my newbie questions was instrumental in reaching this goal. Each person, regardless of their level of success, is supportive and knows what it's like to be new and I'm so grateful to be a part of it.

Dutch – The Late Leader of Bucket List Toronto – He was a pioneer of living life to the fullest and creating a platform for others to do things they've always wanted when no one in their regular lives did. He facilitated 7 years of events! I didn't have the pleasure of meeting him, but I am grateful for people like him for doing what they do. His quote in his obituary is, "When I eventually leave this world, I want to be known as the person who lived, not the person that died." Did he live? Hell yeah! He did and he made sure others did as well. His children will be continuing his legacy through Bucket List Toronto and I can't wait to see what they'll do next!

Matthew Hussey – Your retreat helped put everything I wanted to do to improve myself into words and actions. I knew I had potential trapped inside me, but didn't have any idea how to create a plan or goal. When you taught "thin slicing" goals is when I really gained the ability to take aim. I attended your retreat in 2017, but to this day, I'm still making 1% shifts! I feel I've really grown since that retreat and would do it again to see how much more I can improve and learn by focusing on aspects of the retreat I wasn't ready to explore. When we met, I was impressed by how genuine you are in person. When someone inspires me on screen, but they suck in person, regardless of their message, everything I've absorbed is tainted. Thank you for being you.

Tom Bilyeu – You, sir, have no time for bullshit, no time for whining, and for that, I thank you. You beat to death that if you don't DO something, nothing will ever happen and you can't expect it to. Your use of swear words really drives the message home and it was exactly what I needed, not that fluffy bullshit. I can't fucking wait to see what else you can accomplish.

Simon Sinek – You have this amazing ability to step back to see all the angles in the big picture. In every speech and interview, you've been able to articulate ideas so clearly in ways that are mind-blowing to me. It's helped me be more present and look at things from different perspectives that I hadn't thought of before. I definitely tweeted that you are either fascinating or frightening to date. #notsorry #sexybrain

Kristina Karlsson – Your books, Dream Life Journal & Your Dream Life Starts Here, were gifted to me in an international Secret Santa and it changed everything. My Secret Santa, a young woman from Australia, saw a video I'd posted about having trouble setting goals in a Facebook group and when she was assigned to send me a gift, she knew exactly what to get. You really ask the hard questions in a well thought-out, guided journal. Your books really gave me something to focus on now and for the future. I couldn't have written this book without reading yours!

Yes Theory – Thank you for putting all of the feelings and thoughts I have into words. I've been following your YouTube channel for a while now. I've watched how each of you have all grown uniquely and work hard to be the men you want to become. How you've continuously become more creative and excellent with words has been incredible to watch. Your videos have impacted my life because they're so real; you have this light that makes people who are scared to get out of their comfort zone actually do it. Don't ever stop.

Starbucks – No, this isn't sponsored, but I'm really thanking Starbucks. I wrote almost my entire book at their coffee shops. Great vibes, fellow like-minded customers settled in to work, delightful staff and that damn lemon loaf. Shout out to the shops in Scarborough, Ontario for having an environment that I felt comfortable enough to sit in for hours at a time to write my book. #lemonloafaddict

Table of Contents

FOREWORD

Dear Reader,

Is there something you've always wanted to do in your life that you've accepted that you will never do because you're too busy or feel you don't deserve it?

The New Bucket List by Lisa Vandepol will push you out of your comfort zone and have you setting goals like never before. You will understand what goes into setting your goals, how to follow through and stay motivated. Lisa asks hard questions, but they will help you realize how short life is and encourage you to stop putting your dreams on hold.

It's made me really think about what I've been too busy to do and start making a plan to make that dream a reality. This book will help you do a deep dive into what's taking up so much of your time and how to make time for you. If you've ever said, "I've always wanted to......", this is your opportunity to stop wondering and start doing. Lisa will stop you in your tracks when you say you'll do it later or say you're too busy.

You will also start thinking about what's holding you back and how to push forward. I'm sure you have someone or something in your life that is keep, everyone does, but the author helps you recognize those barriers and bring supportive people into your life as well as keeping relationships with those who are not supportive of your goals. These are all pieces of the puzzle you will encounter in working towards your dream life and this book is a great blueprint to get you on your way!

I feel you will also get value from the section on self-care. Taking care of your physical and mental health is a huge part of reaching your dreams. I mean, if you're not healthy, you can't enjoy them! Lisa gives great examples of how to keep your head in the game and body ready to tackle new adventures.

Lisa's experience with tragedy and fear will help you find inspiration in your own life to set goals and reach them. Her story makes getting out of your comfort zone less scary and more exciting!

The New Bucket List is the book for you if you are feeling stuck and want to make big changes in your life.

Raymond Aaron

New York Times Best Selling Author

Lisa Vandepol

DEDICATION

Dedicated to the memory of Chris Hall.

WAKEY WAKEY!

When you are 90 years old, what are you going to look back on and be proud of?

What will you look back on and regret?

What will you tell your kids and grandkids about that will inspire them or make them laugh?

Are you going to tell them you went to school, got a job and worked every day until you could retire...the end? Is that all there is to your story? No. HELL NO.

Now, I'm not suggesting you take up extreme sports, become an adrenaline junkie and get yourself hurt or killed...but, I'm not saying you shouldn't try new things. If skydiving is something you've always wanted to do, then do it!

In our lives, there is so much opportunity to take a different path it's overwhelming. The elderly have several opinions on regret, but I'm sure right now, you can think of three crossroads that would have made your life very different than it is right now.

That's OK; learn from the past, don't live in it.

You probably had very rational reasonings to make the decisions you did. There's a good chance you made those decisions to avoid change OR you actually took the risk; it either works out or it doesn't, but you'll never wonder 'what if' by taking the path unknown. The unknown is a scary, unpredictable thing, but that's also what makes it so exciting and brimming with new adventures.

Get a pen and paper ready. You'll need it while working through this book, starting now!

Check in with the 90-year-old version of yourself. Picture yourself, sitting in a rocking chair, gazing out the window, reminiscing about the highlight reel of your life. What do you look back on that makes you smile? It's a hard thing to do, I know! I had trouble thinking forward and looking back, too. I know there are things I want to do so badly, I'd be pissed if I didn't get to tell people about it at 90. Write down what you'd be pissed you didn't get to tell people about at 90.

Can't think that far ahead? I've got something more frightening for you: Math. (90 - your age) x 12 = number of months you have left to create your dream life

When I did this, I almost fainted. At the time of writing this, I had 636 months left to live, assuming I'd make it to 90. When I read that number, I could almost hear the clock ticking.

Huffington Post stated that 90% of people have at least one major regret. At least? Yikes! I'm sure you can think of a few regrets already, but you are going to leave them where they are. This is your opportunity to start with a new attitude, being open to new experiences and putting the work into live the life you've dreamt of.

I know what you're NOT going to do; you're NOT going to sit around and wait to die.

You're NOT going to brood over all the things you didn't do. You're NOT going to wallow in sadness for mistakes you've made.

You're definitely NOT going to wonder 'what if'.

The past is behind us and there's absolutely no amount of wondering or worrying that can change it. Re-read the last sentence. Say it out loud. Everyone has something they wish they had done differently and that's OK; no one is perfect, and you're not supposed to be. I want you to take away a lesson, nothing more. No guilt. No regret. No what ifs. I'm going to talk a lot about wasting time in the coming pages and worrying about things out of your control is one of the bad habits you will learn about.

Look forward, because that's the only place you've got to go! You and I are going on a journey through this book. Together, we will work through all the ways to reach our goals and live happier lives. Every day there is a new path to take and I'm excited to see where it leads you. Let's make life better for us, the people we love and the world around us. Sounds good, right?

Let's get started.

Write down your dreams; activities you'd like to do, places you'd like to visit, food you'd like to eat, etc. Be very specific. They can be huge dreams or outrageous dreams or smaller things you just never got around to doing. For instance, one of my dreams is to anonymously pay for a stranger's meal at a restaurant once a month. Nothing crazy, just a feel-good act of kindness.

It doesn't matter how small or big, if it's a one-day goal or will take time to complete, put them all on the list. Don't forget to write down things that you've wanted to do but are out of your comfort zone, like skydiving or stand-up comedy. Getting out of your comfort zone is a great way to grow as a person and will lead you to setting even more amazing goals.

Here are a few more of my specific goals to give you some ideas:

- Go to Brazil for Carnival
- Learn to scuba dive
- Be an extra in a movie
- Run a marathon
- Eat sushi in Japan

Some of my goals can be completed in one day, others will take planning, time and money. You need to create a timeline and set a date. Picking a date is key. Make your list, in no particular order, and get dreaming. Don't forget to think about what you dreamed of having when you were a kid. Adults often forget about those things or brush them off, but if you can remember, write it down. Who hasn't wanted to ride on a fire truck?!

"Lisa, I have a family and a bunch of bills and 18 jobs. It's nice to think about, but I don't have time or money for this."

Mmmmhmmmm. I thought you'd say that. It's funny that when something bad happens, like someone gets sick or your car breaks down, you can, by some miracle, make time! You make time for the bad things but not the good things. Tsk tsk.

There is mental preparation you'll need to take on the task of living your best life. Sounds weird, doesn't it? It's true though. Most people set limiting beliefs on themselves, like being selfless, busy, broke, undeserving or lacking confidence. I will coach you through these limiting beliefs, so you can move forward instead of standing still.

"All the people that will lie in your wake are the people that didn't try simply because they didn't believe they could do it" - Tom Bilyeu

Re-read that quote. It's powerful AF.

In this book, I'm coaching you to be the one causing the wake, not the one caught up in it. I want you to shock people. I want you to do things you had no idea you were capable of. I want you to be fulfilled, happy, curious and excited about life. I want you to believe you can do it and then do it.

Keep your list close, so you can write down anything new you can think of, even if it happens to be someone else's dream or is purely inspired by someone's life. Your list could be huge or small and that's OK! Thinking about all of these goals and dreams will get your creative juices flowing. Later in this book, I'll help you plan how to reach these goals, because we're all going to die, so why not?!

Disclaimer: DON'T DO ANYTHING STUPID. This is not a call to say "Screws this! We're all going to die anyway" and do something dumb. This book is merely a wakeup call to make you aware of it and aware of how to spend your time wisely because tomorrow is not guaranteed, it is a gift. My goal is for you to live your life as fully as you possibly can. No pressure, right?

"When I eventually leave this world, I want to be known as the person who lived, not the person that died." - Peter "Dutch" Schouten.

Don't you want to live life like Dutch? I know I do. I want to be remembered as someone that lived full out and tried my hardest to get others to do the same. I want my life and legacy to inspire you to always move forward, achieve and not just blindly accept the hand you were dealt.

Look at all of the successful people that were dealt a bad hand? Did hey stand by and become a victim of it? No, they rose above it, became accountable, took control and owned it.

I admit, I was a serial blame artist. I would blame my parents, my friends, the weather, traffic, businesses, countries and myself for whatever wasn't going my way. I blamed myself a little, but I never considered my situation my fault. Doesn't that sound crazy? I let all outside influences dictate how MY life played out. Now that I know better, I feel empowered. Everything is my fault and that's OK, but hey, everything is your fault too, good or bad!

Instead of playing the blame game, I'm going to coach you on 'pronoia.' I'm not making words up; it's simply the opposite of paranoia (I didn't know there was an opposite either). You are going to use pronoia to flip the script and make the world work for you and not against you. Along with that, I'm going to teach you how to create positive triggers to creatively influence you, keeping you on the path towards your goals.

Your brain is probably a little weirded out already. Feeling uneasy? You're probably thinking this isn't for you and that, quite possibly, I'm crazy.

"WTF are you talking about, Lisa?"

Buckle up, Buttercup. Humans are wired to keep themselves safe, that's why doing anything outside of your comfort zone is so hard and scary. It's an archaic blueprint, so we need to push through to live amazing lives and grow. I'll give you a little nudge to help you get out there; even a small step is still a step forward!

You and I are going to get your goals in order as well as the cycles in your life. Stepping forward towards a goal is great, but you need to bring the rest of life up to the same level. Perpetually late or messy? Start something and give up? Setting goals and creating a plan is big, but these negative cycles will still hold you back and cause self-sabotage. Since you're reading this book, I'm pretty sure you're up to your eyeballs in this, so I'll coach you to recognize what is distracting you from creating your best life.

Speaking of your best life, what about that body of yours? If you thought I wouldn't talk about health, you are sadly mistaken.

"Lisa...you're not going to make me eat vegetables, do yoga and meditate, are you?"

That's exactly what I'm going to do. Don't like it? Does it sound difficult? Good. This is a small thing to do for yourself that will have huge impact. It doesn't matter how successful you are if you can't enjoy it because you're treating your mind and body like garbage. Exercise, nutritious food and clearing your mind will help you reach your goals and enjoy them.

So far, so good? Good!

Will I be blunt, offensive and probably a little morbid in this book? Yes.

Will I make you uncomfortable? Probably.

Will I encourage you to push your boundaries? Oh definitely.

Time to get living!

Keep that pen and paper handy and read on!

#1 - Screw This! We're All Going to Die Anyway!

1.1 - Let's get crazy! Right? RIGHT?!

Kidding! Accepting mortality does not mean you can be reckless or a jerk or stupid or careless. It means you are going to use your time more wisely and efficiently.

It would be easy to just spend all your money, steal, hurt people, trash the environment and never do anything you don't want to do, just because It's not the apocalypse; it's life. Need I remind you that you're reading this? That means you're alive and you want to lead a happy, amazing, fulfilling life. There's nothing you or I can do about the circle of life, but I encourage you to leave the world a little better than you found it; it's a much better legacy than being 'that guy' that negatively affects it for generations.

I'm not saying reaching your goals is going to be easy, but nothing worth achieving is. In the process of setting goals, don't forget goals to give back. You can give back to the community, soup kitchen, fundraiser volunteering, anything! Be grateful, nurture the soul and know that however you give back will impact at least one person and that makes it all worth it. Life is all about balance; you can't expect something for nothing. I believe the quote is, "The hand that gives gathers."

Let's dive in!

1.2 - Mortality Motivation

Death is a heavy, awkward subject; a bit of a downer. I'm aware my own death is imminent, but there's no way I'm going to let the weight of it bring me down; I'm going to reach my goals and make new ones. Travel to the places I've always wanted and then discover more. I'm going to build the life I never thought I deserved.

Do you want to do those things?

Do you believe you deserve them?

If you don't believe you deserve them, what would make you think otherwise?

What work or penance or whatever would make you believe in your heart that you are worthy of achieving your dreams?

Write it down. There will always be internal and external obstacles, but the internal ones are on us alone to work on and move forward. I believe you deserve a good life and I want to help you get in the mindset to get there.

The whole death thing can be hard to wrap your head around and move forward. I know it can be hard to think of a world without you and the pain the people you love will go through, but this will happen to each and every person forever. Make the most of your life and it will be celebrated. Everyone's life should be celebrated, not just at birth. Are you celebrating your life? Are you going through the motions? Are you making strides to build a better life for yourself, both internally and externally?

I wasn't doing any of those things; I was living a mediocre life. I made enough money to get by in a job I was too smart for. In my relationship at the time, we never talked about what we really wanted because I think we were both afraid of the answer. I struggled to live in my comfort zone and do all the things that other people wanted me to do until the day everything changed forever.

Get ready for the feels…..

1.3 - The Wakeup Call

In high school, I dated Chris for a whole two weeks. I was/am a sucker for big blue eyes. He was so kind, energetic, generous, happy and accepted people just as they were. He also had the overly honest 'I don't give a f*ck' attitude which I liked because you always knew where you stood with him. We parted ways, as teenagers do, and I did not see him for 10 years.

We reconnected over LinkedIn in 2012. He had just gotten out of a long-term relationship and I was quitting my job out of town and moving back home. A big transition for both and we helped each other get through it.

Chris was nursing a broken heart and realizing he had no idea how to date.

I felt defeated; I was moving back to my hometown at 30 with no job and no prospects.

I had no idea what I was going to do. I couldn't believe it when he offered me a contract position where he worked. Wow! Who does that for someone they barely know? Chris did, that's who.

Chris and I worked together for six months and had grown close. We had lunch everyday with his friends and he showed me the local places to eat, because he knew I was a foodie. He was so funny and sarcastic that we laughed every single day. It made me wonder how we didn't stay friends for all those years, but I was grateful for reconnecting.

After my contract ended, I didn't see Chris much; I had found a new job in Toronto, but we stayed in touch. In the following year, he invited me to parties, we'd see each other at food festivals and he'd always ask me for a restaurant recommendation for a date. He'd found a new girlfriend and was ecstatic. I was happy he had found someone that was just as happy-go-lucky as him. He talked about house hunting and was so nervous; it was freaking adorable.

At the end of 2014, I hadn't heard from him. I didn't think much of it; I assumed he was busy falling in love and figuring out how to buy a house. No big deal…

One wintery day, his mother tagged him in a post on Facebook; Chris had a brain tumour. I checked daily for updates. I couldn't stop crying. Nothing like this had ever happened to someone I knew; especially not someone my age! This was stuff that happened on TV, not to people I knew. This was not happening.

A week later, his mom said Chris needed surgery. She said the risks were huge; a "damned if you do and damned if you don't" situation. I couldn't believe it. Was this really happening to someone at the age of 31? It was hitting home that this could actually happen to anyone at any time and it did.

Chris Hall died at 31 of a brain tumour during surgery.

I was shaken to the core. How could this happen? He was only 31! This wasn't fair! He didn't do anything bad to anyone! WHY??

I went through all of the stages of grief, slowly working through the shockwave that he was really gone.

In that instant, a switch was flipped.

I realized all the things Chris couldn't do, but I still could. What was _I_ even going to do?! Time became finite and I was freaking out. I had wasted so much time and vowed I would not waste anymore.

I began evaluating my life. I hadn't even TRIED to do any of the things I wanted to do. Scratch that, I had no dreams, no goals and no bucket list. I panicked. I scrambled to think of something to work towards. I realized I wanted two things: to buy a house and to travel Europe. I told my boyfriend of six years what I wanted to do. He said he didn't want either of those things. I realized in that moment, the man I loved and I were on completely different pages. He and I had never discussed anything past what we wanted for dinner that night.

I couldn't force him to live the life I wanted.

BUT

I couldn't go back to living like time didn't exist.

So, I left.

Within six months, I bought a home, planned my trip to Europe and I've never looked back. Now I think of all the things I never would've done had I stayed with him, selfishly hoping for him to want what I wanted.

It's sad that it took a tragedy to pull me out of the day-to-day daze, but I'm grateful for the wakeup call because I know in my heart, I never would've done it myself. I know I would still be in the exact same place before Chris' passing in 2014. I'd be resenting my boyfriend for holding me back and I'd still believe I could change him for the better (which is totally wrong of me to do). I'd spend every vacation bored at an all-inclusive resort wondering what else the world had to offer and feeling I'd never have the chance to experience it.

FUCK THAT.

In the past four years, I've traveled Europe, Peru, all over the USA and have more travels in the works. I've eaten some crazy foods, gone to some amazing festivals, I've gone skydiving, paragliding, rock climbing and learned things about myself that my 2012 self never would have. I'm learning to push my limits and put myself out there to experience ultimate discomfort followed by ultimate rewards.

You and I have things to do, dreams to accomplish, a world to serve and things to cross off our bucket lists. I don't want to wake up one day and wish I had gone skydiving or traveled to Japan when I had the chance. I don't want you to wake up one day and wish you had done something when you had the chance.

That chance is NOW.

Say YES to pursuing your dreams!

Say YES to trying new things!

Say YES to getting out of your comfort zone!

Say YES to living your life to the fullest!

Say YES to leaving the past in the past!

Say YES to living with no regrets!

This is YOUR wakeup call.

"All our dreams can come true, if we have the courage to pursue them." – Walt Disney

1.4 - SHHHHHH – Four Views on Mortality

When I coach people about living with no regrets, they don't want to talk about it. Many don't want to wake up to the fact that they will die one day and accept that having regrets is OK. It's uncomfortable. It's awkward. It's scary. It's taboo.

The majority of people will push back because it's so difficult to talk or think about. There are four types of people I've come across when it comes to discussing their finite time on earth.

#1 Tick-Tock

The people that accept death as a part of life truly stand out, much like the risk takers, but with a purpose or goal in mind. The people that have been awakened live every day like it could actually be their last. Each day is a gift. They have a goal to reach and nothing will stop them. They wear their passion and talk about it often. It drives them and keeps their hearts full.

Don't confuse this with workaholics; people that are woke have purpose and clear goals. Workaholics can be addicted to the work, chaos, praise or money, not life.

Sadly, there is another group of people that have accepted their mortality but are not driven. It's possible they are affected by mental illness, such as depression, or they are fixated on the question we all ask ourselves: What's the point? Instead of searching for their purpose, they brood over it.

I'm not here to get you into an existential crisis. I will say that everyone has a purpose and if you don't feel there is a purpose for you, you will have to put in the work, try new things and never stop learning to find what gives you drive. I will coach you on finding your purpose through passion later in this book and you'll be surprised at how simple it is!

There IS another possibility of the drive behind this purposeful bunch; a near death experience or witnessing someone die. Psychology Today states that people that experience almost dying have increased self-esteem and lose their fear of dying, but gain purpose. There are several aftereffects of this event, but these are a few of the common imprints.

Witnessing someone pass away can also have this effect, but it can be more traumatic being someone that almost died. One can either feel invincible after surviving or wake up and start living life with purpose.

#2 Hard to Grasp

I was this person; the one that believed death only happened to old people and that I was never going to get old. That's right; I believed aging did not apply to me. As someone who is young-ish and healthy, it feels like 'it will never happen to me.' As my friend, Chris, found out, death doesn't care about any of that. When you see the elderly get very sick, it's still hard to put yourself in their place. It almost seems surreal.

What makes it even harder to wrap your head around is the fact you've never known the world without you in it, so how could it be? Even now I struggle with picturing the world without me in it. Regardless of all the history books, it can be; the world was there before you and I and it will continue afterwards. Life truly does go on.

For people having trouble grasping this concept, like me, they will often need a catastrophic event to kick them into gear. Finding a video, speech, book or article that speaks to them on a deeper level may also do the trick. Getting out of this state was not easy for me and it wasn't fun.

#3 The Invincible Ones

And then, there are the risk takers. It's hard to decide if they accept their mortality or are challenging it. They are gamblers and are most interested when the stakes are high. They are adrenaline junkies: the riskier, the crazier, the better. Most of them don't have long-term goals or a sense of purpose, literally living in the moment.

Living in the moment is something most people struggle with doing, but these people live for it. The risk takers are living in the moment and for the next, but are never satisfied. The risks become bigger, more dangerous and more creative in search of fulfillment. Without a clear goal or plan, they may never find their purpose.

Examples of risk takers would be people in extreme sports, buying a lot of risky stocks in the stock market or placing huge bets at the casino. There are many ways to take risks, but this group doesn't consider the short or long-term consequences. It can put a strain on family and friends when someone like this gets reckless, but the need to take risks never goes away.

#4 Ignorance is Bliss?

When asked, the people that ignore mortality will nod their heads that they are aware they will die, but aren't living their life like it. Those people don't have control of their lives, they have no goal and have not figured out their purpose because they feel they have time to do it later. In other words, they "let Jesus take the wheel" and believe whatever is "meant to be, will be." They believe in luck and that if the life they've always wanted doesn't just happen, oh well. Did Steve Jobs or Oprah Winfrey sit around waiting for their dreams to fall in their laps? No? I guess they were just lucky, right? No? Oh, I guess they worked their asses off to make their dreams come true. So weird. ;)

Another side to those that ignore the idea of death are the people that say they are "too busy" ALL THE TIME. The people that have taken on too much and are taking care of everyone else but themselves. Sound like someone you know? They have stopped thinking about themselves, won't ask for help and have put their dreams to the side so other people can reach theirs. Yes, it sounds selfless, but it's also a little sad. People who do this rarely reach their dreams and then resent the people around them when they finally have time to pursue it and they physically can't. It's too late. This is when regret sets in. It can be hard to give up some control and ask for help or delegate. To make dreams come true, you must make time for them.

Which Type Are You?

Take a look at the people in your life as well as yourself. Which category do you fall into? Which kind of person is your mother? Your boss? Your teacher? Not everyone will show you which type they are; some people are good at hiding it. It's when you have a meaningful conversation with someone that they show themselves. I was surprised at what people showed me about themselves when I dug a little deeper.

Talking to the people in your life about your goals will allow other people to be vulnerable enough to share theirs. That's when you can share your dreams freely and be vulnerable. Be supportive of each other and check in with them to see how progress is going. That is an incredible person to have in your life. Cherish them. Be grateful for them.

When you begin to see all the types of people in your life, it's difficult to let other people live a mediocre life. I've been woke since 2015 and it takes everything in me not to drag my friends and family out of their bubbles kicking and screaming. You can't force them to get it. You can't force them to realize how short life is; please don't try. You can end up ruining relationships if you are pushy and raving about them accomplishing nothing when they're going to die one day; it gets awkward...trust me. Be there and support them. Love them just the way they are. If that's the way they want to live their lives, let them...sorta.

Time to coach you on 'breadcrumbing'. If you've been online dating, you've probably heard the term before, but we're not stringing people's hearts around this time. You will be giving the people close to you just a little information at a time. Tell the people in your life little things about your progress or what you're grateful for to see how they react. Some people are so closed to being present or getting out of their comfort zone, that they could react negatively. All you can do is be there for them when they realize how short life really is. Your loved ones may even tell you that you're crazy, but don't take it to heart. I call them Bubble People; they are trying to protect you and themselves from feeling discomfort. It could also be that they want to feel they have control and by discouraging you, you'll do what they want. It's not a crime for someone to believe everyone should live life like they are, but that's their life, not yours.

When your friends and family complain about something not going their way, and they will, ask questions to make them realize where they could've done something different; it gets them thinking from a different point of view. I've received some (LOTS of) push back, but also received "I didn't think of it that way." The person that didn't think of it that way is open to new ideas and new ways of thinking. You will find people with a growth mindset, open to change and improvement, and people with a fixed mindset, afraid of change and who are never wrong. Often people will blame the world for things not happening for them, rather than blame themselves for not making them happen. Think about how you got to where you are right now. Did you create it or was it created for you? Proactive or reactive?

A perfect example of this came from someone I've worked with. We were sitting in the lunchroom eating when my co-worker blurted out that she hadn't accomplished much in the past few years. Confused, I asked, "What did you want to accomplish?" She just stared blankly at me. Then, I asked, "What did you expect to happen in the past few years?" She said she expected to be making a lot more money, but didn't want to go for a certification because she already knew what she needed for her job. Then I asked her, "Did you apply for higher paying jobs? Or ask for a raise?" She said no. I asked her about going for that certification, but she was still up in the air about it. Sound familiar?

She didn't set a goal; she expected it to just happen because she worked hard, knew her stuff and felt she had earned it. She also saw other people getting ahead without asking. As we all know, life doesn't always work the way we'd like it to. If you want something, you have to literally ask for it, make a plan and execute. Sometimes the work you do doesn't shine the way other people's does, so it's your duty to bring it into the spotlight.

Are you, or someone you know, afraid of succeeding? Does it make you uncomfortable knowing that you could achieve something great? She knew that without that certification, she wouldn't have the right to ask for a raise. I think some people are afraid of asking for what they deserve and want to be recognized without asking because they feel asking can be seen as greedy or selfish. Sounds like a little self-sabotage, doesn't it?

#2 Regret vs Money vs Time

2.1 - No Stone Unturned

Since my friends live "too far" from Toronto, I had to find a way to get out of my comfort zone and do things I'd never had to opportunity to do before. On meetup.com, I joined a group call Bucket List Toronto - Because our friends stopped doing fun stuff too. When I saw the tagline, I was in!

Dutch, the late creator of this group, noticed after six years running this group that skydiving was still #1, but the cost was holding may people back, including myself. In the spirit of crossing this whale off of everyone's bucket list, he made a payment plan. The event was set up months in advance and he asked us to pay $50 every 2 weeks until the $300 price tag was paid off. This was so manageable! I then realized that I can do this for ANYTHING I've always said was too expensive. You can do this too. How did we not think of this before?

So, if I hear you saying, "I can't cross something off my bucket list because it's too expensive," well, then you don't want it enough. You are going to die one day. Are you going to stop yourself from experiencing something amazing because of money?

Newsflash: You can make more money; you can't make more time.

Getting out of your comfort zone or conquering fears doesn't have to cost any money at all. This is where creativity kicks in.

Afraid of heights? Find a rooftop patio or balcony and take a look around.

Afraid of snakes? Find a petting zoo for children.

Afraid of water? Go to a lake or swimming pool with a friend.

Afraid of strangers? Ask a stranger what time it is or for directions.

Be safe. Practice. Get over your fears...for free.

Say yes to empowering yourself.

Say yes to getting over your fears.

Say yes to crushing those fears that have plagued you for your entire life.

My fear was water. I was the kid that cried when they got splashed and clung to the edge of the pool. When I went on vacations, I would reassure whomever I was with that it was OK if they went on water activities without me.

I now know I missed out on so much by letting this fear drag me down. It had control.

I had accepted that activities like cliff diving, scuba diving and parasailing just weren't in the cards for me.

At the age of 36, I walked into the change room at the gym and there was a poster that said, "Learn to Swim". I thought to myself, 'It's a sign! ...and it's an actual sign!' I reluctantly emailed the swimming teacher and gave her every excuse why I couldn't learn to swim.

I wear glasses...I won't be able to see.

She told me where I could get prescription goggles for under $30.

I'm too scared...I can't do this.

She's taught adults who have almost drowned and they did it.

I'm too old for swimming lessons.

She has taught people in their 60s how to swim.

I was out of excuses.

Like me, you probably need a little push to get there. My swimming coach, Patti, was that person for me. She knew how far she could push, but she could also see that I was frustrated with this fear. I had no excuses left, all I had to do was show up and that's all you have to do. Just. Show. Up.

2.2 - Regrets of the Elderly

So, let's get back to the start of this book; being 90 years old and remembering the past. The website, Power of Positivity, states these as the top 10 regrets of the elderly.

1. "I Wish I Lived For Myself More."
2. "I Wish I Didn't Work So Hard."
3. "I Wish I Didn't Hold Back My Feelings."
4. "I Wish I Stayed In Touch."
5. "I Wish I Was Happier."
6. "I Wish I Cared Less Of What Others Think."
7. "I Wish I Didn't Worry So Much."
8. "I Wish I Took Better Care Of Myself."
9. "I Wish I Didn't Take Life For Granted."
10. "I Wish I Lived In The Now."

Read these and think about which ones you already regret. Many of these you can remedy now or learn from at this age rather than brooding over them at 90. I don't know about you, but there are at least three of these that I have regrets for. Which do you have regrets for already? How are you going to stop these from being negative thoughts in your later years?

Let's do a brain dump and get these nagging thoughts on paper. Grab a piece of paper and write down your regrets you have right now under each elderly regret. Writing anxious thoughts down is a great way to clear your mind of clutter. I want you to have a clear mind moving forward to focus on your plan and improving yourself in the process.

Being distracted by things you cannot change doesn't serve you, so I want you to let them go. (This is also a good trick to use if you have a lot on your mind and can't go to sleep. Simply do a brain dump and sleep soundly!)

Here are a few examples from my brain dump:

1. If I had just told people how I felt, my life would be completely different.
2. I'm the worst friend. I've lost touch with so many amazing friends. I don't try hard enough.
3. If I had not cared what everyone thought, I'd be happier. My life would be different because I wouldn't be trying to please my family and try so hard to get their approval.

Can you relate to these? Getting these thoughts out of my head and on to paper has helped lessen how often I think of them. I know I can't change the past, but I can change how I react to these going forward. I read these back and know I will try my best not to make these mistakes again.

Analyzing this list as if you were 90 is a great method of looking at a goal and working backwards; I'll go over this more later in the book. Right now, you can stop some of these from becoming regrets and lift the burden now, so you can live your life more freely. Be present, not distracted with regret, worry and what other people think. Like I said at the start; learn from the past, don't live in it.

You and I need to fulfill our dreams before we're spilling our regrets to our caregivers in old age. As our time is finite, you need to achieve your dreams while you physically can. Unfortunately, there comes a point when your body starts to turn on you and there may be things you still wanted to do, but your body can't handle them. There may be no hiking Machu Picchu or skydiving or mountain climbing, so start now. Be adventurous while your body is healthy and keep that body healthy, so you can experience as many physically demanding goals as possible!

Having new adventures creates incredible memories you can relive over and over. Material things are nice to have, but don't always create that lasting memory. If one of your goals is to own your dream car, how will you feel when you first drive it off the lot? Amazing, right? What about a year from then? Will you still have that feeling? The feeling shiny things give us fades over time, but the experiences you have will replay in your mind and be just as amazing. Once you feel the difference between enjoying shiny things and extraordinary experiences, you'll crave more experience over craving more stuff.

At your funeral, no one is going to talk about how many cars you had, the house you lived in or the clothes you wore; your friends and family are going to talk about what you said, what you did and most importantly, how you made them feel. In the end, material things don't really matter. Let's be real, they're nice when you're here, but you can't take them with you when you pass away. Focus on moments, not materials.

"You'll never see a hater doing better than you." - Unknown

2.3 - Memento Mori & Distractions

Society tells us that it's morbid and creepy to talk about mortality and the media definitely doesn't help. I was sheltered from it, even when someone was actually about to die. No one explained what happens when someone dies or why, so I would just see the body at the funeral and lots of crying people. Since I saw how upset everyone was, I wasn't about to ask about it because it seemed like a bad thing, not the natural event that it was. Even simply saying that when you get old, you die and go to Heaven would've sufficed. Growing up, death was not celebrated, it was feared.

There's nothing wrong with being scared of death; it's perfectly natural. No one truly knows what happens or what it feels like when you die. It's funny that with all the science and research, it's still a big question mark. Every person and religion has their own opinions about it, but I guess we'll all have to wait and see! Whether it be Heaven, Paradise, reincarnation or simply just peace, 70% of people believe there is something after this world.

Fearing death does not mean to live in fear; the grim reaper isn't sitting on your couch waiting for you to come home. Knowing that your life is finite liberates you from monotony and putting things off. It makes you proactive and allows you to want to achieve your dreams without guilt. Who in their right mind guilts people who are going to die? No one. Those people who want to guilt goal seekers don't fathom that they, too, are going to pass.

Did you know that in some cultures, they remind you that you will die to keep you in the present moment? Not a widely celebrated part, but it exists.

It's called 'Memento Mori'; it translates to "remember your death." It's not meant to be a downer, quite the opposite. Stoics, and even Christians, use this to remind each person to live life to the fullest and be grateful for each day. Marcus Aurelius wrote, "You could leave life right now." and the Bible says, "So teach us to number our days that we may get a heart of wisdom." Psalm 90:12.

The Romans also practiced a form of memento mori. After a victorious battle, the soldiers were treated as gods, but during the victory procession, a slave was assigned the task of repeating to the leader "Remember you are mortal" over and over.

Memento mori's purpose is to encourage you to live now, be present and treat each day as a gift. The Stoics remind themselves constantly to not waste any time and give meaning to each day. I know it can be a challenge to give meaning and gratitude to each day; it might not seem like all rainbows and sunshine, but the sky is blue above the clouds. As someone that struggles with being grateful on a crappy day, I get it. If you are able to buckle down and write three things you are grateful for each day, YOU ROCK. I highly recommend keeping a journal or calendar to write at least one thing you are grateful for daily. Even when you're having the worst day, there is always something and you will find it!

Another difficulty of giving meaning to each day or working towards your goals is technology. After getting home from work and eating dinner, I get on Netflix, YouTube and social media. There are so many distractions! By the time I'm getting ready for bed, I realize I didn't accomplish a damn thing since I got home. Not cool.

Insert guilt here. :(

I could've spent that time doing ANYTHING, but I chose to do nothing. I chose to push my dreams off to another day. I chose to waste time I cannot get back. I mean, it's not going to kill me, but I didn't use that time to improve my life or anyone else's. The Stoics would not be pleased!

As society has become safer and scientific breakthroughs make people live longer, talking about death is taboo and considered morbid...because not talking about it means it won't happen, right? Death is not celebrated, it is feared. People talk about death like it only happens to the elderly, the ill or the unlucky. People live their lives like they have all the time in the world and they can just do things 'later' or 'one day.' This mentality drives me crazy!

How would you live your life differently if you found out you had one year to live? What about six months? Three months? One month?

This could happen to you or someone you love at any moment. How will you live your life knowing that? Will you put more effort into your dreams? Will you say yes when you would normally say no? Will you say no when you would normally say yes?

I've stopped wasting my time and stressing out over things I don't enjoy. The book 'The Life Changing Magic of Not Giving a F*ck' by Sarah Knight has liberated me from these exhausting burdens. For instance, I no longer attend musicals, children's birthday parties, baby showers, wedding showers or jack & jills. I'm not a jerk about it, but I simply can't make it and that book will show you how. I'm sure you have your own list of events or tasks that stress you out, take your money and waste your time. I'm not willing to part with any of those three things, if I don't have to and neither should you. Be firm and move on. You've got better stuff to do with your time, damnit.

This does not make you selfish. Stop thinking like that. There are times to bite the bullet and do the thing you don't want to do, but you are not required to say yes to those things 100% of the time. Stop feeling guilty. Get. Over. It.

Are you one of those people that feel wanting something for yourself is selfish? Do you deny yourself getting what you want so you look better to other people? Are you too scared/shy/embarrassed to tell people what you want? Do you think your dreams don't matter?

If you answered Yes to any of these…Oh boy, do I have several words for you.

You probably know what I'm going to say, but I'm going to tell you again and again until you get it.

You matter.

Your dreams matter.

Your happiness matters.

Don't ever forget that.

Why is it OK for other people to chase their dreams, but not you?

Oh wait. It's NOT ok?

You mean everyone else isn't more important than you?

Yeah, that's what I thought.

I want you to think about that. Really think about it. What makes people so much more special than you that they can do it and you cannot?

I ran into this when I thought about writing my first book, but it didn't come from my self-doubting brain; it came from an outside influence. When I told my family I was going to write a book, they told me they didn't know what to say; they didn't know anyone that had written a book. So, I asked them what made other people so special that they could write a book, but I could not.

They had no answer. It occurred to them that they did not know what qualifies someone as an author or how to become one. So, why would I listen to them? Are any of them authors? No. Are they an authority on what it takes to be an author? No. Yet, my family was still able to put that doubt in my head, thus claiming control of my goal and that book never got written. I recognize the influence I allowed them to have over my dream and I will never let anyone do that again.

The same goes for any dream. What makes you less worthy to obtain that goal? The people that reached their goals probably weren't 'qualified' to others, but they worked harder than anyone that was 'qualified' and that's how they reached their goal. People like Oprah and Richard Branson didn't listen to the people that doubted them. I'm sure you know their stories, and look at them now.

Think about your dream.

Why is it perfect for you? Why do you feel you are destined to do it? Why is there no possible reason that you can't do it?

Certain dream jobs do require formal training. I don't care how much you want to be a doctor, without med school I don't see that happening. It's not that you're not worthy of achieving that dream; you're just not qualified YET.

Will people tell you you're crazy? Probably.

Have those people achieved their dreams? Probably not.

I say this time and time again; misery loves company. I run into this almost every day, whether I've signed up to run a race, gone on a date or decided to write a book. No one wants you to be happy or rise above them; they want you stay at their level or lower forever. A lot of people are jealous, have low self-confidence or cannot think outside of their bubble. They cannot accept that the people working for their dreams outside of their bubble are not freaks of nature. The goal seekers are not special; they just want it more and it shows.

Our brains are programmed to keep us comfortable and safe. A lot of people project that onto other people when they feel someone is wandering into an uncomfortable or unsafe situation, even when, in reality, it's not. You are exploring the unknown and moving towards something incredible and they are not. Everyone has fears, but you will never experience something incredible and new if you don't face them.

I know it's hard to digest that your people believe they are looking out for your best interests, but are also trying to keep you on the path THEY believe is right for you. It's not their life and they are probably trying to make you relive the life they currently have because it's comfortable.

Everyone believes their way is the best way. It's not wrong, it's just THEIR way, not yours.

"If not now, when?" - Primo Levi

2.4 - Got Resources?

So, what would you do if you could not fail?

That's one hell of a hard question, right? Would you run a marathon? Dance? Open a business? Become a doctor? A pilot? Buy land and fill it with animals from shelters? Apply for the job of your dreams? Write a book? Get married? Write them all down!

Everyone I ask this has the same response, "Buy a lottery ticket." Well, THAT was anti-climactic. If that was your answer, try this question:

If you had all the time, money and resources in the world, what would you do?

Travel? Have a ton of kids? Buy a zoo? Buy an island? Save the rainforest? These are not easy questions to answer. Take some time to think about what you would do; this question is not simply black and white. What dreams have you been unable to fulfill because of time, money or resources? Write them all down too!

Look at your list of dreams. Make sure they are all positive. "Getting out of debt" has the word 'debt' in it which doesn't make anyone tingle with excitement. Change that to "Have spending money for new shoes" instead of hoping that 'one day' you can get those super cute shoes. Be as specific as possible. The more specific your dream, the clearer and more attainable it is. Once you have that very specific, super exciting dream nailed down, you can break it down into smaller steps and begin to work on it.

Anyone that has done something great has sacrificed for it. What will you sacrifice to reach your goal? Will you give up your daily Starbucks? Miss out on concerts? Cook at home instead of going out? You have to use your resources wisely to get what you want! If you're not willing to give up that night out instead of working on your dream, think about how you'd feel if you never achieved that goal. Giving up something for your dream should not be viewed as punishment because reaching that dream is going to feel so much better than that latte.

Determined to write this book, my friends wondered if I had been abducted. I would get invited out to dinner, events and even just to hang out, but I declined almost every invitation. If I went to every event I was invited to, I'd never complete this goal of publishing a book, so I sacrificed my social life to do so. They thought I was crazy to write a book, but I wasn't going to let them deter me. This was MY goal...crazy or not.

The big push was when I told everyone when I planned on publishing it. It was September of 2019 and I decided January 2020 was when I would publish. I wasn't done writing the book yet, but everything else was in place. The website was mostly done, the cover was ready and social media accounts were active. Setting that date put me into high gear and telling everyone was what I needed to get the book done. From that date, I was able to set milestones to ensure I'd actually get it done in time to be edited, formatted and printed for the launch.

Setting that date was clutch. Setting those milestones sealed the deal.

Give yourself a timeline. I personally like to work with three-month goals. What can I reasonably accomplish in three months? I can learn Spanish well enough to survive in a Spanish-speaking country. I can learn to swim. I can get into the habit of meditating daily. Circle the goals on your list that can be completed in three months.

My first three-month goal was Spanish. I was going to Peru and my goal was to order food in Spanish. I downloaded Duolingo and off I went. I set my alarm 15 minutes earlier each day and did my lesson. When I was in Peru, I was ordering my cerveza, my agua sin gas and asking for my la quenta por favor like a boss. I was amazed at what I could learn in just three months!

Our time on this earth is finite, so three-month goals are less daunting that a five year plan. You can take a goal that will take longer than three months and break it down into three-month goals as well. So much less pressure and way less overwhelm. Setting goals isn't meant to overwhelm you, it's meant to give you drive, excite you and fulfill you!

Long-term plans are more fragile because things change. You can't let disprupted plans within the first year derail the entire plan causing you to give up, that's why breaking them down into smaller goals is the way to go. From there you can adapt the next three-month goal accordingly. Pretty cool, right?!

"If you don't sacrifice for what you want, what you want becomes the sacrifice."

\- Jay Shetty

#3 – It's All About Mindset

3.1 - Labels

Everyone labels themselves and accepts labels from others; whether it's true or not, it creates an excuse. Do NOT tolerate labels from yourself because of other people. Just because someone says you're late all the time, doesn't make you that person forever and it doesn't mean you can't change. Habits are not permanent; it's not a personality trait or a scar, and if you want to change bad habits into good habits, you will have to put effort into getting out of that pattern.

If you're often late, set your alarm (NO SNOOZE) earlier and get your things ready the day before.

If you're messy, set a timer for five minutes and clean as much as you can at the exact same time every day.

If you have trouble getting to the gym/library/class, make a consequence for it. Get an accountability buddy and have them create a task you want to avoid each time you don't go, like $5 per class, 10 burpees, or singing/dancing in public, etc.

Break the cycle. Do the damn thing.

I've been labeled as several things in my life and so have you, but I'm not going to sabotage myself into being late all the time because I was labeled as "the late one." Don't let those negative labels get into your head because the people that labeled you will never remember all the times that you arrived right on time. Those people want to keep other people down below them. Those are the people that are never wrong and blame everyone but themselves. Those people will never live a full, happy life but you will because you know in your heart that their opinion, in the scheme of things, doesn't mean a damn thing.

What are they doing that's so great anyway?

Look at the people who refuse to leave their bubbles. They may be happy there or they might be miserable. They sit in their bubbles, blaming the world for everything instead of getting off their butts and actually doing something about it. Do you know these people? I bet you can pick out five people in your life right now that do this, and it's so normal. If you can't think of those people right now, you will start to notice the blamers as they whine about things they can absolutely change but choose to complain about instead.

You, on the other hand, are aiming for bigger, better things and they will come if you work for them, not wait for them. You are done with complaining. You are done with labels. You know you are in control of your life. You learn from mistakes and vow to never make that same mistake again. You are not trapped by their bubble. It's up to you and no one else to set that goal and go for it. Focus, focus, focus! The only person that can stop you is YOU!

Do you have a message that is demanding to get out? Write that down! Your message may not be dialed in, but write down what you truly believe in that would make people's lives better. Some talk about relationships, trust, honesty, faith, meditation, mental health, exercise, fears or about a specific field, like fishing, chemistry or makeup, etc. Everyone has something that triggers them into a passionate rant and that just might be your message.

I tried to write books before, but my heart wasn't in it. I had no idea what my message was. I had labeled myself as a short form blog writer and determined that books were not for me. I also labeled myself has having a short attention span with nothing important to say. I thought there was no way I could write something long enough to be made into a book, yet here we are.

3.2 - I Am Who I Think You Think I Am

Ponder all the people you admire and want to emulate. Write down why you admire them and which of their characteristics you wish to have. Is playing it safe one of them? Blending in with the crowd? Being average? Not likely. These pioneers beat the odds, think outside the box, ignore the naysayers, work their butts off, push against the status quo to chase dreams that no one believes they can reach. THAT is why we admire them. They KNOW without a shadow of a doubt what their goals are and that they are going for them, full throttle, in success or failure.

Take all of those characteristics you admire and be that person. Be the person for other people to admire and be inspired by.

Let that sink in. Is there someone in your field that makes you feel that way? I think every field has that top dog everyone wants to be like, or makes others give up because they are so damn good at what they do. You can become that person too, if you put in the work. There will always be someone better, smarter, faster and more successful than you, so don't try to be THEM. Be YOU, but better. Find your niche and know your audience. Zone in on it and take it!

Start setting goals within your niche and writing out your plan. If you feel you won't stand out in your field, find one thing that differentiates you from the rest and use it to find your audience. Amplify that one thing and become an expert in it. Keep dialing in on your niche and get hyper-specific, so you can become an expert on it.

To be honest, I didn't really know that was how to start when I had realized my purpose, even though it seems so obvious: research! I started to set those small goals, like finding like-minded people. I talked about my goals with the people in my life I see regularly and followed through by holding myself accountable because I knew my friends and family would ask. I couldn't believe I was creating these minuscule goals and it was actually working; I was moving forward. It became an addiction. I started to feel momentum. I even started setting more goals.

That's when I started asking people about their goals, dreams and fears. I kept asking them, "Why not?" when they would say they would never do something due to fear, being busy or had never achieved that goal just because they never thought they could. I pushed them to set a date for the small goals to give them a taste of what it feels like to do it. I'd follow up with them. It felt good to see them move forward and that's where I started to find my niche.

If I hadn't set up a plan, I never would have attacked a larger goal: time to write a book, damnit. This was a scarier goal and something I'd never done, so it was challenging to write out the steps. I watched training videos and read articles on how this is done to make my plan. You should do the same when taking on something completely new. There is a ton of information, and mentors and experts that can help push you in the right direction.

It's time to finish what you start instead of giving up halfway because it's challenging or seems impossible. Stop worrying about what others think and keep those discouraging thoughts away. Failure is when you stop trying. Stick to the plan!

"Will you get so good, you become the excuse that other people use not to try?" - Tom Bilyeu

3.3 - Around We Go - Cycles

Cycles are evil. They're negative habits and tendencies that hold us back and bury us with distractions. Examples of negative cycles are not listening, forgetting to take out the garbage and treating your car like a closet. Not devastating, but not useful.

Everyone has habits and cycles, both good and bad. The bad ones are the hardest to stop; they enable our excuses and are a complete distraction. Stopping those cycles will help you be more productive and think creatively. I believe the quote is "Doing the same thing over and over expecting the same result is the definition of insanity." Let's not be insane. I want you to clean up; organize what's in front of you to help you clean up and organize what's in your head.

Is your bedroom constantly a mess? Is your car full of junk? Do you never finish any projects? Can you never find what you're looking for? These are cycles and they must stop. Clean up your home and it cleans up your mind. Stop the cycle of living in disorganization and you will be able to focus on your dreams. Living in a mess is a distraction that makes you feel guilty for living in it. And you stare at it day after day thinking, 'Man, I've really got to clean that up.'

List time! Look around. What needs attention in front of you right now? Messy desk? Dishes in the sink? Shoes all over? Recycle bin overflowing? List five things that need your attention and make a plan of attack. As you cross these things off the list, you'll start to see other things that need your attention and add them to the list. Once you're satisfied, the list can be used to maintain this sanctuary instead of living in a tornado aftermath.

Depending on the size of the mess, start small; I started with one shelf. I cleaned off that one shelf, threw some things out, found things I was looking for and gave it a good dusting before putting things back in a more organized fashion. It felt good. It was a small thing, but it was a start.

From there, list in hand, I would choose what I was going to clean up each day and I could instantly think clearer and gained a sense of pride.

You know...I really feel like dusting today...said no one ever. Cleaning up your home or your mind isn't glamorous, but neither is the path to your dreams. Things will be difficult and messy and sometimes downright destitute. You will have to do things you don't feel like doing, like going to the gym or cooking a healthy meal. Clean up your home, keep your body healthy and your mind clear to continue to move forward.

There will be things on the list you've been avoiding FOREVER. You will probably do everything on that list plus the new tasks you've added and STILL avoid that one. If you don't do that task, how do you expect to have the drive and perseverance to live your dream life? Did you think this was going to be easy? Sounds silly, but it's a pattern to break. It's true that if you don't attack this one stupid household chore, you're sabotaging yourself to stay right where you are because there are more intimidating, scary, difficult tasks ahead, so stop telling yourself you'll do it later.

"You're never going to feel like it" - Mel Robbins

3.4 - Pronoia!

"Lisa, WTF is 'pronoia'?"

Glad you asked! Paranoia is the feeling that the world is out to make you fail. Pronoia is the feeling that the world is going to help you succeed.

Never heard of it? I hadn't either. Instead of feeling like you're being sabotaged by the forces that be, feel like the world has a plan for you and everything will work out as you strive to achieve dreams. Your dreams ARE achievable, no excuses, but sitting around, letting time pass you by isn't going to make them happen. Once you put the wheels in motion, you will be unstoppable because the world wants you to succeed.

Remember how I told you that our brains are wired to keep us comfortable and protect us? Well, there's a loophole. Sort of.

Our brains create the state of 'boredom' for a reason. I know no one likes being bored, so what's the point? The state of boredom's purpose is to get us moving and do something with purpose. I'd never thought about why it exists, but now it makes sense.

While your brain wants to you to be productive, it does still want to protect you. Way back when humans were hunters/gatherers this had great purpose, but now that we don't have sabre-toothed tigers to worry about and food is readily available, that type of protection is a little unnecessary.

Boredom now is generally filled with mindless crap involving a screen or plain old sleeping. Your mind is trying to tell you something and this is when you should listen to it. To do this, you'll need something that interests you and keeps you focused, something that stimulates the mind or body.

There are several factors that Psychology Today describes regarding boredom, like waiting in an airport or a lineup, but I'm talking about boredom you have absolute control over. I'm not going to get into the nitty gritty of all the different scenarios, like Netflix and daydreaming, because there are different levels of boredom! I feel that once you harness the boredom you have control over, you'll be able to better use that down time, like that time between work and dinner or after dinner and bedtime.

Boredom is dependent on energy or arousal. Get your mind out of the gutter already. Geez! If your brain has high energy or arousal, you will get bored more quickly. A little meditation can lower your energy level and your frustration with being bored or you can jump up and get your blood flowing. Changing your physiology is the perfect way to remedy boredom. It's an opportunity to get shit done, don't waste it!

Take one of your goals and start breaking it down into smaller tasks. That's where this boredom comes in handy. You can tackle some of those tasks or do things you don't feel like doing, like cleaning, but let's face it, you're never going to feel like it. Why wait?

#4 – Dreamkillers

4.1 - The Dreaded Self-Sabotage

No one needs any help from outside influence, self-sabotage is probably the number one killer of dreams and we do it to ourselves. It sounds absolutely crazy to me that we would stop ourselves from doing what we've always wanted to do, but we are all guilty of doing it.

Let's start with the biggest culprit: procrastination!

Nah, we'll do it later. Kidding!

We all make up excuses in our heads about why it's OK to put something off or do it later. You KNOW completing these tasks is good for you. You KNOW it will bring you closer to the life you've always wanted, so why go against your better judgement? Why not do it?

I'm too busy.

I'm not good enough.

I don't feel like it.

I'm tired.

I'm scared of being successful.

I'm scared of reaching my goals.

Think the last two are a little deep? They are 100% accurate.

The key is to break down big tasks into smaller ones. Those small tasks are much less daunting and time-consuming thus less intimidating to attack. Rewarding yourself for completing these tasks is an excellent way of staying on track.

Here's the formula: Only do *the thing you love* while doing *the thing you're avoiding*.

Such as: Only listen to your favourite songs while exercising. Only go to your favourite coffee shop while writing a chapter for your book.

If you're going to reward yourself for taking those steps forward, there must also be consequences for not getting out of your own way. Having someone keep you accountable, like going to that coffee shop with someone else that wants to get work done or hitting the gym with a friend. You can keep each other on track and that is powerful.

If you're lacking like-minded friends in your real life, then you'll have to take the wheel or find other ways online. You can use a service that will charge you money if you fall off the wagon. Scheduling your time to put in the work is also a great tool to stop procrastination; you blocked off that time, you might as well do something with it!

4.2 - Little You, Big Dreams

What did you dream about being when you were a kid? Did you want to be a firefighter? An astronaut? A teacher? The President?

Did you notice that at one point in your life, you stopped dreaming? I know I did. There was never a profession I wanted to be as a kid, but I did dream about things I wanted to have and things I wanted to do.

I dreamed of having a bunch of dogs and a bunch of cats.

I dreamed of going to the highest point and looking at everything around.

I dreamed of meeting the teen heartthrobs from TV shows and radio. (NKOTB OMG)

Hell, I even dreamed of being on TV.

I want you to write down the dreams you had as a kid. Did you achieve any of them? Were they too lofty to attempt or actually impossible? Like, dreaming of having a third eye or living on the clouds.

What happened to all that? Did you dismiss these dreams as childish or crazy, or did you stick with them? Why haven't you done it?

If "time" and "money" are your answers to this, then you need to remind yourself that you can make more money, but you cannot make more time. Start saving money, if that's what you need to get the ball rolling. Have the bank automatically transfer a specific amount of money into your dream account. Look at how long it will take you to save to accomplish that dream and set a date. Too many people dismiss their dreams when they get caught up in life. It isn't until they cannot do something that they realize that they dreamed of doing it their whole lives but never made the time. This is where regret kicks in. Yuck.

You are going to die one day; are you OK with NOT experiencing one of your dreams?

That's another heavy question. Look at your list. I'm sure there are dreams on there that would be awesome, but not mandatory. Thinking about what you'd be OK with not doing is a great way to prioritize your list. There are a few things on my list I'd be pissed that I didn't do. What are those for you?

Talk to an elderly person about their life. Even asking about jobs they had or people they dated before meeting the person they came to be with long-term will give you insight into regret. I don't really recommend asking them directly what they regret, but they'll tell you with a distant look in their eyes as they recount a story of their youth.

Living in the age of dating apps, I asked an elderly woman about dating in the 1940s. She told me about dances, theatre shows and live music spots that were the popular places to go. She told me about one boy and as she looked to the window, she said, "It just wasn't meant to be." I'm still not sure if that was good or bad, but do you want to look back at your life when you're 90 and regret not taking a chance? She took the chance and dated the boy she met on the streetcar. Do you take the chance when you see a cute boy or girl? Or do you let them get off the streetcar?

4.3 - Obstacles

Pick one of the goals you've chosen; one that can take some time but is attainable. Write out the steps you know you need to take to get there. Step by step, from emailing someone to picking something up at the store to learning a new skill. Every single tiny step. Throw in possible obstacles you think you may encounter. ALL OF IT.

Sitting there staring at your plan? My favourite excuse was always, "I need to do THIS, but I don't know how." HA! Nice try. No need to give up because of one step; just Google it. Include experts, authorities and friends in your list to ask for advice or help. Sounds easy, right? Do it! You'd be surprised at how many people want to help you and you don't even know it. Especially those who are successful have a need and want to help others.

Also, you can't expect people to just know what you need, nor do you know all the resources or skills they have; don't assume they don't have any. When I told a friend that I was writing a book, she immediately offered to proofread it for me because proofreading was something she did all the time at work. I had no idea that my friend had this skill and it made me wonder what other skills my friends and family had that I didn't know about.

If you put the need out to the universe, help will come to you. I truly believe that. Like, when I put out into the universe that I needed to save money, the universe gave me a four-week cough/cold. Did I save money? Yes. Was that how I wanted or planned to save money? No. The universe is funny like that, so be very SPECIFIC.

Being specific is another challenge for you. Everyone wants to be successful, but success is defined differently by everyone. I cooked dinner without burning the house down or getting food on my shirt; does that make me successful? Apparently, that outcome is pretty common...who knew? I made it to work incident free and worked all day, then made it home safely. Is that success? Is getting a job, any job, the definition of success? For some, yes, and for some, no. Being specific about your goal is key. The universe wants to help you, but you need to tell it exactly what you want.

One of my dreams I wrote down when reading, 'Your Dream Life Starts Here,' was to travel, but the book wasn't satisfied with that. How often do you want to travel? Who will you travel with? Where do you want to go? What do you want to do when you're there? That book really pushes you to make very specific goals, and I get it now. Creating your goal by being super specific is the easiest way to write out the steps to create your plan. You'll know exactly when you've reached a goal if you really dial it in.

Do you want to open your own brick-and-mortar business? Where do you want it to be? What do you want to sell? When do you want to open it?

And the most important question…WHY do you want to open this business?

Figuring out your 'why' will keep you motivated and on course. Not starting with 'why' may lead you down the wrong path.

4.4 - Learning From Mistakes

Learning from mistakes is NOT the same as regret. It sucks that you messed up, but what did you learn? Learning is the best part of making a mistake, big or small. You've got that mistake out of the way and now know what won't get you to where you want to be.

I want you to turn regret into something useful rather than wasting your time dwelling on the negative. From each and every mistake, failure and regret you can learn, and learn about yourself, making sure you don't repeat it. Did you find that speck of positivity in it? What process or habit are you putting in place so it doesn't happen again?

If you never make mistakes you don't learn or grow. You'll never reach your very best without a few battle wounds. All successful people have failed hugely in their lives and that's why there are so many successful people behind the most moving and inspirational quotes. They didn't make up those quotes because they are smart or great writers, they said these lines because they lived and breathed the lesson behind it.

What quotes inspire you? I've included some of my favourites throughout this book, but there are thousands of them. When you find some that really hit home, write them down. I have a whiteboard in my living room and one by the door with quotes on them to keep me motivated and in a positive state of mind. I find they keep me on track, especially when I start to lose hope or get lazy.

Having inspirational quotes and people around are a great way to keep a healthy mindset as you're surrounding yourself with positivity and encouragement. If you're unable to find like-minded people around you, I recommend getting inspiration from amazing content creators on YouTube and podcasts. There are speeches and interviews by very inspirational people that can help you keep your head in the game. We want our dreams to come true and to create the lives we've always wanted, so don't get off track. These people know what it's like to be in your position; they kept on track and pushed until their passions and dreams were in front of them. You can do the same thing; there's no magic trick. There's no fast track. Success comes from plain old hard work.

#5 - TIME TO GET UNCOMFORTABLE

5.1 - Pushing Through

Discomfort is not a bad thing. Discomfort means you're trying something new, out of your element, in an unfamiliar situation, something you might be terrible at, something you may or may not even like. Discomfort is experiencing something you've never experienced before. It's something you will talk about, brag about and write about because it will leave a mark.

Have you ever thought about why you are afraid of something? Have you thought about why something makes you anxious or uncomfortable?

I was catching up with a former co-worker and I told her I was going skydiving. She immediately said, "I'd never do that! Heights are not my thing!" Before I could get a word in, she told a story of her husband going parasailing in the Caribbean and called it "stupid" and "crazy" followed by an epic tale because it didn't look safe, she was scared he'd get hurt, etc. So, then I asked..."Did your husband have an amazing time?" She said yes. So, then I asked, "Would you have had this incredible story to tell if he had not gone for it?" She said no. So, was this really a bad thing? This is when she went into a rant about all the things that COULD have happened, instead of focusing on the part where her husband had an amazing time and he was so glad he did it.

I asked her if she had something bad happen to her to make her dislike heights. She said no and that she and her cousins would jump off a barn into piles of hay as kids. Confused, I got to the Google for some answers.

It turns out, as you get older, you are less open to new experiences. I am fighting this inevitable urge with everything I've got.

Now that I know this is a real change as you age, I see it everywhere. Relatives and co-workers, whom I know were badasses at one point, are now rigid, stubborn and safe. When you are young you are motivated to do things that will improve your life, but as you get older, you're motivated to keep things consistent and smooth. I'm sure this is part of your brain trying to keep you safe, but it can also keep you from living fully. While both mindsets are good, neither should stop you from achieving what you want. When you instinctively say no to something, ask yourself why. Is it really that dangerous or crazy? Are you being shy or giving in to anxiety?

Always be safe, but don't forget to check if it's your brain trying to protect you from discomfort or if it is actually unsafe. You brain will be screaming NO at the thought of discomfort every time, but I don't want that to hold you back from a new, possibly amazing, experience, so make sure you understand that discomfort doesn't always mean danger. Pushing yourself to get over a fear, or dancing in public, are definitely uncomfortable, but they are not putting you in harm's way.

Did something happen in the past that is holding you back? Or are you playing the what-if game? There are two sides to a what-if game; what if this fails and what if this is the most amazing thing you've ever done?

Your brain is wired to keep you safe. Your brain's primordial instinct is to avoid anything that causes discomfort. Back in the days of hunting and gathering, your brain would sense danger and activate the fight or flight mechanism; the same way a poisonous food will taste bad. This instinct stayed with humans throughout evolution and causes us to stay home rather than go out, eat the usual foods over trying something new, not going on a rollercoaster or parasailing or anything regardless of how it appears.

Everything has risks. EVERYTHING. Driving. Walking. Eating. Working. Skydiving. Going to a doctor. Not going to a doctor. There are risks everywhere. So, are you going to live your life in a bubble? Are you going to shelter yourself and everyone around you from living an amazing, unique, fulfilling life? Are you going to deprive them of the stories they are proud to tell when they are 90? Or will they tell stories of playing it safe and working until they retired...The End. Are you going to be THAT person that makes everyone else feel like crap for taking a risk just because you won't?

I just don't see you being that person. You want more and that's why you're reading this.

Are you going to be the person that asks, "Can I come?" Are you going to ask friends and family how their goals are coming along? Are you going to be their cheerleader and keep them accountable? Be an accessory in people succeeding, not the party pooper, even when it's something you're not interested in; everyone's passion is so unique! It's a great opportunity to ask questions and learn about someone else's goal to understand, support and grow.

Just because you feel you've done things right because your life is going OK doesn't mean that's the right path for everyone. This is YOUR path...right down to the way you cook your eggs. Other people cook them differently, but that doesn't make it wrong. Many people try to steer others into their lane since they feel it's the right way, just because it' comfortable to them. That's just plain narcissistic. You can give advice or guidance when asked but stay in your own lane.

Encourage risks. Encourage failure. Encourage learning. No one skates through life without failing at something and learning lessons from it, and you know it. Life does not give you participation ribbons for playing it safe. Life does not give you incredible stories to tell others by doing what others think you should do. Life gives you the opportunity to try again and again.

5.2 - Get Over It

If you have a fear of something specific, like heights or dogs, take small steps to get over that fear. It's so freaking empowering to conquer that fear and once you do, you feel like you can do ANYTHING!

The feeling of conquering a lifelong fear is like no other. In everything 've done in my life, it's a euphoria that I'd never felt before.

I know this because I did it.

Water was my kryptonite. I had a crippling fear of going underwater ny entire life. I've been on several trips where water activities were nvolved, and I sat out of Every. Single. One. I missed out on snorkeling, arasailing, scuba diving, waterfalls and every water park ever.

After crossing several things off my goal list, I looked at my list of goals and there it was, still sitting there, staring me down; I was sick of itting on the sidelines watching everyone have fun and push their limits. The universe knew I was ready. There was a sign at my gym for adult wimming lessons and it was actually happening. I was ready.

In the moments of arriving at my first swimming lesson, I learned omething new about myself. I learned that I had hung on to the identity of he non-swimmer for so long, I was almost afraid to let it go. I would lways make special arrangements for myself while everyone else went to he water park, or I'd find some way to avoid it. I didn't know what life vas like as someone that knew how to swim, as someone that could say ES to water.

You can say YES to getting past your fear and letting go of that dentity. I cried in front of 15 strangers at my first swimming lesson, but I till went back. It was embarrassing and it sucked, but I wasn't going to let ear win. I needed to shed that identity of not knowing how to swim. I was eady to walk away from fear.

I started small; just get in the damn pool. One step at a time. Just get 1. Do nothing but get into the water and just stand there. Breathe. That's ow every dream, goal and the journey to conquering a fear begins; just et in. If you don't get in, you'll never know what could happen.

Be open to that opportunity. Be open to that change. Be open to the nknown.

It took me 36 years to get in the damn pool. Do I look back on everything I missed and wonder? Of course I do, but the water is still there and I can still go experience all of the things I sat on the sidelines for. Do wish I had done it sooner? HELL YES. Was I ready to conquer my fear of going underwater 10 years ago? No. I had not experienced mortality motivation, so I stupidly thought I had all the time in the world and would learn how to swim 'later.'

I guarantee I never would've taken those lessons if I hadn't woken up to the fact that it's something I may have never actually gotten to do. I'd still be the one watching everyone else experience diving, snorkeling handstands and yelling "CANNONBALL". I do still hide from splashing but I can snorkel! I cannot believe I'd missed all that beauty, but am grateful to see it now.

When I told my father I had learned how to swim, he just hugged me.

Since this is a new skill I've acquired, I haven't told anyone really When an opportunity to swim comes up, I'm there. When I come up from swimming underwater across the pool to look at everyone's shocked faces it makes it all worth it!

You can conquer a fear, just like I did. It won't be easy and it won't be fast, but it's completely doable. Just breathe. Just get in the damn pool.

5.3 - Just Say Something!!

As extroverted as I am, I'm still an introvert at heart, so I going out of my way to talk to strangers wasn't something I was comfortable or confident in doing. At a wellness retreat, they taught us about putting yourself out there more. The coach, Matthew Hussey, said, "Just say something!"

Right after the retreat, I felt like a new person. Everything I had learned was fresh in my mind and I was ready to put it into practice. I had a grand opening of a brewpub to attend, so I thought this would be the perfect time to see what I could do.

Assessing the room, I saw a kiosk for a brewery I had been to. I had only intended to take a photo for Instagram. The beer slinger, whom I didn't know yet, was chatting with some people I didn't know when I walked up and he offered me a sample. I could've said, "No, thank you," but I didn't. I said, "Oh, I'm just grabbing a photo for Instagram." He said, "You're on Instagram? We're all on Instagram!" gesturing to the people he was talking to. "Let's get a photo!" In that moment, I was thrust into the group of influencers in the beer community that are now my good friends!

Had I meekly declined the beer or not walked up at all, I'd have been denied the opportunity to get to know these amazing people. Also, knowing these wonderful beer enthusiasts widened my network which opened up even more opportunities in the beer industry where my network was very small. All of this happened because I said something. Wow!

Not only did I simply say something, but I also blurted out the truth. The phrase, "The truth will set you free" has never been more true. Making up excuses or lying is only going to pull you away from your goals, your colleagues, your friends and family. It bogs down your brain and distracts you. Being honest brings a calm to your thoughts, just knowing you don't have to make up excuses or more lies to cover old ones. If you screw up, admit it. If you like something, say it. If you don't like something, say it, but don't be a jerk about it or brush it off.

No more cover up. No more lies. Liberate your mind!

4 - Time is a Tickin'

Picture it...you've won a shopping spree, but you have no idea how long it is...it could be five minutes, it could be an hour, it could end any second. Excited, you dive in and begin to fill your cart grabbing everything in sight...quickly at first and then a little slower, because you don't have a plan and haven't figured out everything you really want, not to mention, you don't know how long you have.

At what point in that shopping spree are you going to fill your cart the fastest? The beginning? Will you give it your all the entire time? Or do you give it everything you've got when a timer suddenly counts down from 30 seconds?

Think about that. Is that how you're going to live your life? Coast through, being picky, choosing wisely, until a doctor tells you there's a specific amount of time left? Is that when you decide to start crossing things off your bucket list?

Why wait? Waiting is a precursor to the regret you already know you will have. Don't let self-sabotage creep in. No one is stopping you. You have control. Take the first step. You will never regret trying, you will always regret NOT trying. The old phrase, "Actions speak louder than words," has never been so true. Put your dreams into motion.

Is it scary? Yes.

Will you be giving the middle finger to regret? Also yes.

I find that my friends and family who don't realize they will actually die someday try to keep me in the bubble. When I'm going to embark on an amazing challenge or adventure they bring up every excuse for me not to do it. I'm sure some of these sound familiar...

It's too expensive.

That place is dangerous.

The flight is too long.

You don't speak the language.

You won't like the food.

What if you get hurt? Or sick?

What if? What if? What if?

These are all things I used to tell myself every time I was going to fly to a country I'd never been to or try something way out of my comfort zone. That little voice still creeps up when I'm checking out trips, but all it takes is a little research and asking other people who have been to the place and everything is settled. The world is so big and so small at the same time. Explore it. Don't miss out because of other people's bubbles. Do your research on what you want to do and get out there! Do not get sucked in!

The irony is that these people that are trying to keep you safe/sheltered/boring act like they've never done anything crazy, adventurous or fun. Oh, they've got stories and you've probably heard them. When they tell you an epic tale of the past, ask them how it made them feel or if they regret it. Most of those stories end with, "I can't believe I did that." I understand that the people that care about us want to keep us safe, but do they really want to keep us from living and experiencing life? You know when you're doing something potentially stupid, so the result of that is on you; but if you're simply traveling to a new country or jumping out of a perfectly good plane, that should be encouraged. Better yet, see if you can get the Bubble People to come with you!

Are your Bubble People still not on board? That's ok, mine weren't either; they literally pretended it wasn't happening when I went skydiving or traveled somewhere exotic. It's annoying and a bit tiring, so I thought I'd try a new approach.

If it was something I knew they'd freak out about, I'd talk about stories of other people doing the things I wanted to do, their why and how it made them feel. Letting them know how it had inspired me to do the same. From there, I'd explain how doing that activity or travelling to that place would make me feel.

I began routinely I talking to the people in my life about their bucket lists, asking them about how they were following their dreams to see where their heads were at. Since I brought it up often enough, they knew it was something I was passionate about. It's important not to be pushy about it; some people are uncomfortable with the thought of being uncomfortable.

If they pushed their dreams to the side, ask why. So many people don't pursue their dreams because they think they have time and they'll get round to it one day. Sadly, most of my friends and family aren't on the Mortality Motivation Train yet, but I was surprised at how many were pursuing their passions and I had no idea. Turns out, they also kept things to themselves because their friends and family thought they were crazy and didn't understand why they did the things they did.

We had been keeping each other in a surface level relationship. I, for instance, had a surface level relationship with Jeff, my own brother! It was always meaningless conversation about how things were going, the weather and whatever or whomever was in the immediate area. It wasn't until Jeff went through a life changing experience that he woke up and saw him come out from the haze.

Now we talk more than we ever have in our whole lives. He's always been a wild child, but now it has purpose. Doing something new or backpacking in South America with no plan (OMG!) is exciting, not reckless. He has discovered gratitude and is so much more aware of what is important and what is not. Jeff has come a long way and I'm so proud of him!

He did this all on his own, but I know it was easier having our dad and myself on the same playing field to talk to about it. Validating how someone is feeling about something they love or hate, or their dreams and goals makes a world of difference. I wish I had that at the start, but I didn't know my family or friends truly understood, and I never would have if I hadn't started talking about my goals and asking about theirs.

Surface level conversations do absolutely nothing for me, but I understand their purpose. The people in your life that stay in a routine and don't do anything outside their comfort zone will have trouble relating to you. You probably make them uncomfortable because they don't know what to say, and when you ask a question about what they've been working on they don't have an answer. Your driving energy puts them off balance and they're not sure how to take you or respond to what you're saying. That's when things get weird and a surface level conversation about how amazing the food or weather is will save your butt from further awkwardness and put them at ease. It will keep that person in your life and not cause them to avoid you...which has happened to me. :(

"You know you're going to die one day, right?"

Out of pure frustration, I've sprung that question upon people that lidn't seem to get it. Not the best approach. Using the "you could get hit by a bus tomorrow" analogy, while true, doesn't hit home. Even using something specific in their life to describe the risks they face every day, like crossing the street to go to the bus stop or their long commute to work doesn't always resonate. Anything could happen any time, but since nothing has happened in all these years they believe it has been validated that nothing WILL happen. They believe that deviating would be the cause of something happening, so they stay the course.

.5 Perspective

Perspective is everything. If you ask an acquaintance what's been going on in their life and they tell you they've added some rare stamps to their collection or put a new fence in their yard or went to a museum about coffee tables, don't judge them because it's not exciting to you; it's exciting to them and that's what's important. "Tell me something exciting!" I say to friends. It leads to immediate confusion and then panic to think of something they think you would find exciting, but that's not the point. My intent in asking them about what's exciting in their life has nothing to do with me, it has to do with going below the surface and creating a more meaningful conversation.

Don't know what to say? Here's a trick psychiatrists use...just repeat back the main point of what they said in the form of a question!

You: It's been awhile! What have you been up to? Anything new?

Friend: Not much really. Went to a coffee table museum yesterday. Pretty cool!

You: Coffee table museum?

Friend: Yeah! They show the evolution of furniture over the centuries!

You: Evolution of furniture?

You get the picture. It will help you be engaging and make them fee you are taking interest in their interests. Not to mention, it's WAY bettei than talking about the weather! It's a great way to learn about someone and helps you have something to talk about next time you see them.

Encourage them to try more new things or improve their homes o expand their collections because it's what makes them happy, and the world can always use more happy people!

Accept that they are content with their lives. Not everyone strives fo being content, but some people nail it and don't feel the need for more I've met a few people that were content, even though they had come close to death, it made them even more content with their life and grateful fo what they had. I was a little jealous as I have an insatiable need to do more, they don't feel the need, but if they experience something new, they go with the flow. I struggled to admit being content was a goal too.

Use perspective to keep positivity in your life. Use it to bring positivity to others that don't believe their life is very exciting. Use it to help others see the other side to a story.

#6 – Work That Body

.1 - Self-Awareness

You've heard how athletes visualize themselves winning when they prepare to play the big game or begin a competition? You can use that technique in your life as well, not just sports. You should be visualizing yourself taking the steps to attain your goal for just 30 seconds o a few minutes every single day. If you can, have a visualization board vith pictures of what you want your life to look like.

My visualization board is kind of...well, it's kind of everywhere. I have peg board with photos in my bedroom, I have a whiteboard with nspirational quotes in my living room and my gratitude wall by the TV. I ike to have reminders of my dreams everywhere I look, so I can focus on hem every day. I will have the life I've always wanted and I'm not giving p, neither should you.

I want you to notice when you're self-sabotaging yourself. The xcuses, "I'm too tired" or "I don't feel like it" or "I'm scared" are going to op up. Note when this happens and how often it happens. The only erson you're going to listen to is you, so if you fall into your own trap, ou already know you're going to feel guilty about it.

Skip the drama. Ditch the guilt. Neither of these things serve you nor vill they make your life better. Noticing it is a huge step to becoming nore self-aware. Being self-aware is a huge step to staying focused and ositive.

If you find yourself in one of those self-sabotage moments, stand up. 'hat's it. Just stand up. Get a glass of water. Move around to change your tate. Now that you're up, you might as well...do something...right? Even the littlest things count, even if it's not towards your goal, but just closing a cycle. Wash dishes. Dust. Take out the garbage. Go for a walk. It will do wonders for your mood and energy level. Once you feel more energetic go back to that step that you're avoiding and DO IT. No waiting, no excuses. You won't regret it. The sooner you finish, the sooner you'll get closer to that goal. The sooner you complete that step, the sooner you'll know if that was the right step to take. Move forward!

Did you waste a little time? Did you let not feeling like it get the best of you? Give yourself a break. When you've been focused and on task for a while, you can burn out. Watch some Netflix, walk around the mall or meditate. Taking a break does NOT mean giving up, it means giving yourself a chance to recharge. Don't wallow in guilt, wondering what you could've gotten done in that time.

6.2 - Healthy You

Take care of yourself damnit. You can work on living the life you've dreamed of all you want, but if you're not living a healthy lifestyle, you won't be well enough to enjoy it. The idea is to prolong the enjoyment as long as possible! That's why giving yourself a break is just as important as eating healthy and exercising.

Does eating healthy and exercising sound a little boring? Kinda, but it's worth it. The rewards outweigh the struggle. I've seen people treat their bodies like a garbage can and instead of living an active enjoyable life into their 60s, they've had surgery after surgery, take tons of pills and cannot live alone because they smoked, drank alcohol often and put terrible food into their bodies.

No, thank you.

If you workout for 30 minutes twice a week, it's literally 1% of your entire week. Think about the percent of time you waste scrolling through social media and watching cat videos: I guarantee you it's more than 1%. You DO have time for this, but you must get off your butt and do it. Put the phone down and go for a walk or to the gym or find a workout on YouTube or find a workout buddy to drag you out. This is important. I will help you calm your mind and make you feel DAMN good regardless of what you did. But you've got to do something and you've got to start somewhere. There is no shame in asking for help from someone that has been working out a long time. They don't expect you to workout as hard as they do, but they can definitely help you start.

In my original online presence I was a food blogger, and I LOVE food but I've definitely eaten a lot of crap in my day. I'm not talking about depriving yourself of all that is delicious, but don't eat it all the time. You know what they say: moderation is key! Sweets and French fries are my weakness, but I've learned to choose something else or only have a sample size portion. Deprivation will lead you, and me, to falling off the wagon hard. Don't deprive, just sample to keep yourself, and me, on the right track. IF, and only if, you have the willpower, you can have a cheat day instead of having a sample size a few times per week.

Did you fall off the wagon, eat an entire pizza and wake up in a puddle of melted ice cream? Learn something from that. How did it feel to break a promise to yourself? Pretty crappy, huh? What can you do to help you not do that again? Have a contingency plan, like phoning a friend or going for a walk in a weak moment.

What do you do after falling off the wagon? You begin again. Don't give up because of one mistake. Remember, this is when you learn from your mistakes, not let them define you.

When you were a baby learning to walk, did you give up the first time you fell down? Did you decide walking may not be for you? No, you got back on those chubby baby legs and tried again. That's what you are going to do with everything on your way to your dream life; try again.

You know what the most important body part is to make you reach your goals? Your brain. Many of us forget to take care of that blob of fat between your ears, but it's so so important. The importantest actually. ;)

I came across Dr. Daniel Amen, a psychiatrist who has scanned over 100,000 brains, and preaches taking care of your brain. Your motivation, mood, focus and memory are all affected by brain health…And I though eating reasonably well and exercising was enough. Nope!

There are foods, like walnuts and fish, that have the nutrients you brain needs to keep all of your hormone levels good and each part of you noodle working properly. I want you to be laser focused on planning you goals and working towards them. Your diet is something you have complete control of, so I want you to make sure you're nourishing you entire body.

I had no idea that when I have trouble focusing, it could be because o my diet. When this happens, I look up the brain food Dr. Amen suggest and think back to see if I've been slacking in that area so I can correct it.

Another undeniable way to care for your brain is to not get hit in the head. Obvious, right? Activities, like football and soccer, can cause impac to your head that can lead to damage. It might not be catastrophic brair damage, but it's enough to do a little and repeating impact to your hea adds up.

"There is nothing in a caterpillar that tells you t's going to be a butterfly."

— R. Buckminster Fuller

6.3 - Meditation

Meditation had never crossed my mind until I read '10% Happier' by Dan Harris. His story is about his career as a reporter in war torn areas PTSD and how he recovered. An entertaining book describing the power of meditation and how Dan used it to calm his mind and handle his ego. His book spawned a meditation app which is how I got started in meditation.

It's an amazing tool to reset your thinking and create space in your mind. Overthinking can allow you to talk yourself out doing something because you're living in the past, and that is distracting you from moving into the exciting future ahead of you.

Meditation helps you be present.

Like right now. Be here. Now. Stop thinking about what you're going to eat later.

It's just you and this book, baby.

Meditation, even for a few minutes each day, calms the mind and relaxes the body. I had no idea how shallow my breathing was until began listening to guided meditations. Guided meditations are great for beginners, because the speaker will tell you what to focus on which distracts you from feeling like the meditation's taking an eternity.

I didn't realize how many moments in my life I wasn't present for Everyone is guilty of this. Our brains are full of thoughts, feelings and plans. The world around us is chaotic. All of this happening at once can take you completely out of that moment. Being self-aware is key.

Even now, I still catch myself on my phone instead of enjoying what is actually happening around me. When I catch myself reaching for my phone, I put it away...even though everyone else is on their phones Practice it. Lead by example and others WILL notice.

Muscles need a rest day and so does your brain. You can't stop thinking for an entire day, but you can certainly give it a few minutes each lay to just be still and quiet. The thoughts of laundry and that you're lmost out of milk will creep in, but just let them gently float away and get ack to the breathing.

There are so many benefits! I can be a bit quick tempered when the ight button is pushed. Meditation has given me the presence of mind to ake that extra second to respond, so I don't react with something I'll egret. I have thanked my lucky stars for that extra second; it has saved my utt! I can note my thoughts, take a step back for just a second, like a third arty, and take a good look at them before acting or reacting.

I encourage you to include meditation into your daily routine. To help ou get those creative juices flowing and emotions calm, it's best to do it efore you begin working on something important, something that equires focus and lots of brain power. Meditating will help keep your iind and body calm to use that energy on deep work.

Ideally, you would get your mind into a 'flow state' to get the most out f the practice.

Lisa...what the hell is flow state?

Glad you asked. Let me ask you this...

Have you ever been so immersed in an activity that time flew by and ou had no idea?

Have you ever been so focused on a task that the outside world ceased exist in that time?

Have you ever been so passionate about an activity that you were ompletely fixated on the here and now?

You've been in flow state...and you didn't even know it. Ha! Ieditation helps you get out of your own way and get into a flow state on mand.

Meditation is just one way to enter flow state. For the purpose of taining goals and creating your dream life, goal clarity, creativity, high consequences and serious concentration in a team environment are al excellent ways to get there. Flow state is especially powerful in a team environment, when the ideas are flowing and the communication is clear Activities, like running and swimming, can also do it, but I don't think you'll want to dive into work right after that!

6.4- Let the Ideas Flow

Now that you've gotten rid of distractions, kicked those negative cycles to the curb and feel like a million bucks, let's put that newfound brain power to work!

I keep a pen and paper on me at all times, so I can utilize times o boredom when I have little control over the situation. I will journal, write down ideas or just draw. James Altucher, speaker and entrepreneur, told Tom Bilyeu that writing ideas every day is his routine. He said it doesn' matter what the ideas are for, just to work that idea muscle will help you come up with better and better ideas. So, when I'm standing in line at the grocery store, I'll look around and whatever catches my eye, like tabloid magazines, I'll think of ideas for them, like crazy new headlines or new professions for celebrities. Not all boring times can be productive times but make the most of them!

If you're still dragging yourself to do something, find an emotional trigger. What's an emotional trigger, you ask? It's something to make you feel a certain way instantly and it's a fantastic tool.

For instance, while I'm loud and hilarious, it's hard for me to get motivated to go out with my friends. I'm so cozy on the couch, cat in my lap and Netflix is on, but my social life is beckoning me. I start to get ready, very slowly and I end up arriving late. Not cool.

Instead, when I'm not feeling like going out, I have a specific song to play that gets me off the couch, gives me energy and gets me dancing. All it took was a SONG to get me out of my blanket burrito and I only discovered the song in 2017! It's helped me FEEL like going out AND I'm not late all the time...still some of the time, but not every time! (It's a cycle I'm still trying to stop!)

Amazing, right? We all have these triggers and you don't even know it, so I want you to be aware of what things, like music, give you energy, keep you focused or put you in a great mood. Write them down or make a note on your phone. You are literally figuring out how to manipulate yourself. It sounds crazy, but it works!

What's your song?

Another trigger I have is for writing. Again, the blanket burrito is deadly when it comes to productivity. In that state, I couldn't be bothered to write, but will feel guilty about it if I don't, so I quickly write something mediocre and return to burrito state. For my best work, I retreat to a local coffee shop. A change of venue always helps me get the creative juices flowing! However, it can start to get a little expensive or if the weather is bad or I'm feeling under the weather...that doesn't mean the writing doesn't have to get done. I got coffee to go one day and realized it wasn't just the coffee or the venue that was the trigger, it was THE CUP.

At the coffee shop, I would get my drink and settle in; once the drink was finished, so was I.

When Canadian winter hits, sometimes going out is not an option, so I bought a cup from the coffee shop, identical to the one I always order, for under $5. Now when I need to be productive and focused, I bust out the cup, fill it with whatever I feel like drinking and work away until it's empty. It's absolutely perfect!

What are your emotional triggers?

What tasks or moods do you need one for?

There are triggers for everything from going to the gym to productivity to getting on stage to getting out of your cycles like procrastination or being late. Begin to notice what yours are and write them down. Also write down what activities or moods, positive or negative, you don't have buttons for and keep an eye out for them. It can even be a reward for getting through a negative situation or dealing with negative people. I mean, we all keep junk food in our desks for a reason, don't we?

You and I have covered a lot in this chapter. You've got a great list of goals and dreams going, so don't forget to add to it when something comes to mind. Keep it around and visualize yourself achieving the couple you've chosen to work on. We're going to be working on those and helping you push yourself towards them while fighting off self-sabotage. Onward!

6.5 - Picture It

In many of the books I've read it was recommended to have a vision board. I mentioned before that I have one and it's just a great passive reminder of what you're working towards. Use photos, clippings from magazines, quotes and positive words to paint a picture of your dream life. I mean, if you can't spend 30 seconds visualizing what your new life looks like, how will you know when you've reached it? Jack Canfield recommends keeping it to one theme per board, so if you run out of space make another! Don't remove photos of goals you've already reached, keep them as reminders that you CAN reach your goals. I love this!! It's a great way to keep the momentum going!

I made my first board after seeing this suggestion on Oprah when was 20. I thought it would be easy; I stuck a photo of some Ikea furniture on it and a super fit woman then called it a day. After a couple years of it sitting there stagnant, into the closet it went. My vision board sat in the closet for 15 years.

Recently, I was at my parents' house and remembered to dig it out so could make a new vision board. I was floored; several of the photos I had put on the board had come true. For instance, I now owned my own home, have done some traveling and I often run and go to the gym.

It made me wonder what else I could've accomplished if I had kept up on that vision board. Hmmmmm.

When I returned home with my board, I just stared at it. What the hell was I going to put on this vision board to help me visualize my dream coming true? I went back to my 101 dreams list in my Dream Life Journal. I realized most of my goals were experiences, not material things. wanted to travel a lot and experience other cultures, so I printed out assport stamps to decorate my peg board. If your dreams aren't actual hings to post photos of, think of something that represents your goal, like did.

Take a minute every day to look at your vision board and picture ourself achieving those goals. I smile every time I look at the photo of a nicrophone on a stage and my heart fills with pride that I did public peaking for the first time. I'm filled with excitement when I look at all ne places I plan to experience. Put photos on your vision board that excite ou and keep you focused.

In addition to photos, I have a sentence of a future goal written in the resent tense. I say it out loud when I wake up and before I go to bed. our affirmation could be something like, "I own my own business dog rooming in Chicago as of January 5, 2025." Create an affirmation that uits a big goal, one that you plan to make a living on or something you lan on obtaining, like buying oceanfront property. Write it down and add to your vision board. Make sure it's in the PRESENT TENSE not the UTURE TENSE. Repeating this to yourself in the present tense makes it el real and programs that truth into your brain.

"Nothing happens TO YOU in life Everything happens FOR YOU." – Ed Mylett

#7 – PASSION

7.1 - How Do I find My Passion?

It's much simpler than you think. As you go through your day or experience new things, note what gives you energy. That's it.

"Lisa...WTF? That's it?"

No really, that's it. When you are doing something that gives you energy rather than draining it, THAT is a passion. There are things in your life that do this already, but you haven't thought of them that way or maybe you haven't noticed. When I'm at an improv class or singing and dancing alone in my condo where no one can see me, it gives me great energy and happiness. It's true that for me, these things are not viable career options, but I want you to note the feeling you get when you do something that gets you excited. Remember that feeling, so when it happens again, you will notice it. Passion can truly spark from anywhere!

There are activities that give me energy and I had never noticed; I always thought they were fun but didn't see the difference between regular fun and energetic fun. To me, rollercoasters are regular fun, but dancing to my favourite music is energetic fun and I feel I could do it over and over; it's an activity where time ceases to exist.

I want you to note the difference in your life. For some, cleaning until your home is spotless gives you energy. Dressing up and looking your very best can give you energy. There are so many things that give you that special kind of energy; keep an eye out for them!

Once you get a feel for that energetic fun in daily activities, take note at work or in your hobbies. I know hobbies really should be energetic fun, but I've had hobbies that were only kinda fun and sometimes even felt like work! YUCK! Are you eager to build airplanes? Are you delighted to show off your Excel skills? Do you get pumped to give presentations? That's the energy I want you to notice.

Honing in on that passion to turn it into your dream profession is the first step. Keep that pen and paper handy, or app for note taking on your phone ready. Be aware and be present when you have that surge of energy and take note of what you are doing or talking about when you feel it. Enjoy it and allow the energy to flow, but don't forget to write it down!

Not all passions are career-worthy, like my passion for petting all of the dogs I see, but it's still a great feeling that I can go back to. You can also tap into those mini-passions for energy when you need it.

Remember how I talked about skills being transferable? The skill that gives you energy is where you want to begin improving. Learn more. Practice more. Ask for feedback. Work to make it your actual job rather than part of your job or a hobby. Be the expert or authority on that specific thing. You can then train others on that thing or even write a book on that thing. You could give a speech about it at a conference or for your company. There are so many ways to find, use and enjoy your passion, but you've got to find out what it is!

Your big big goal is to find your purpose, best described as ikigai. Never heard of ikigai? It's a Japanese word composed of two words; ik (life) and kai (the realization of what one expects and hopes for). In good times and bad, your ikigai is what drives you to get up every morning with purpose.

It's broken down into four elements in a handy Venn diagram.

What you love (your passion)

What the world needs (your mission)

What you are good at (your vocation)

What you can get paid for (your profession)

Finding a passion that checks all of these isn't easy. I'm sure you have few skills that check off a couple of these boxes, but not all. For instance, I'm good at being organized and I'm paid for it, but I don't love it and I don't believe it helps the world in any way. However, I'm good at encouraging people to get out of their comfort zones, I believe the world needs it, I'm paid for it and most importantly, I love it.

Being good at something and being paid for it are where the majority of the world sits. I rationalized it by making life outside of work exciting, but it wasn't enough for me; I knew I needed something more fulfilling to help people, not just myself.

Get that pen and paper out. Make five columns; Action, Passion, Mission, Vocation and Profession. Under Action, I want you to write down all the things that spark energy, hobbies, what you're good at, your current job and your dream job. Go through the list and put a checkmark under the heading each one fulfills. I'm good at having a positive attitude, so I would put a checkmark under Mission, Vocation and Passion, but not Profession. See which actions fill the most categories or which ones have potential to check all those boxes.

You might find something already on your list that you had not considered pursuing before! You may also find something that doesn't fill all of the categories yet. Is there something on that list that you love, the world needs, you're good at it, but you're not paid for it? Many people fall into this because they feel they can't ask for money or it's 'just a hobby' or it's a gift for them to give. While all of this may be true, money is a catalyst to reaching more people with your message. Money is not evil and doesn't mean you're being greedy by asking for it.

I'm THE WORST at asking for money...even if it's not for me!

When I worked at a manufacturing company, customers would call to ask for pricing. When I told them the price, as confidently as I could, I would cringe, just waiting for them to freak out. It took everything in me to not fall into agreeing with them that it was a lot.

What I learned is that money means different things to everyone, so a low dollar amount to you may seem high to someone else. You never know who you're talking to when it comes to money, just know what the product is worth and stand by it. Be able to describe all of the benefits that make your product worth the price you've given them. If what you're offering is worth the cost to that person, it's a no brainer. If your potential customer doesn't believe the cost is worth it, move on. It's a valuable lesson!

7.2 - For the Children!

Hey Parents! I'm not a parent, but I wish I had started noticing passions and skills when I was younger. I would've loved for the people closest to me to notice what I'm into and encourage me to pursue it further rather than doing it for fun. Hindsight is 20/20, so keep a notebook with your children's interests and what they want to be when they grow up. I'm sure these will change yearly, so keep it updated! There are so many things I loved when I was younger that I completely forgot about. I'm not saying they were all passions, but they brought me joy!

I feel like I'm late to the game, but I'm still in it! Don't hesitate to give your kids a head start when they don't know what to pursue themselves. It's a great reminder of what gives them energy and maybe it will help them find their passion in life earlier than you and I!

Besides a photo album, it will also give your children insight into who they were as a child. It may reignite a part of their personality they had lost. Were they a curious child, but now a cautious adult? Were they a shy child, but now dominating conversations? It's interesting to see how people evolve as they grow, and I think it would be incredible for them to see how they've changed as a person since they were small.

7.3 - Why THIS Dream?

'Why' is a big question when it comes to creating the life of your dreams.

If the reason you're starting a business is just to make money, you'll never be fulfilled. What you are selling is proof of your why and money is the bonus. Money is not what puts the fire in your belly; it's showing the world your purpose and seeing how it affects people in the best way.

Your 'why' is what drives you to reach your dreams. Your 'why' is what fulfills you and makes your heart full. Your 'why' is the impact you want to have on the world.

Your 'why' isn't only business related. The reason you want to reach any of your dreams is very personal, but I still want you to think about it. For each dream you pursue, think about why you're doing it.

Why did I go skydiving, you ask? I wanted to challenge myself. I don't have a fear of heights, but when you're at the open door of a plane staring down from 10,500 feet, you question your sanity in doing this. Upon exiting the plane, it was pure freedom. I wanted to feel the rush of free falling and see the beauty of my country the way the birds see it.

When I told the people close to me I was writing a book, they said I was crazy. If I had started the conversation by telling them about my experiences, how they made me feel and that I wish I had known this earlier, they would've bought in. Once they were in, I could've told them I was writing a book and to them, it would've made sense.

Did I do that? No.

I said I was writing a book and when I told them what it was about, they didn't get it and said I was crazy. Clearly, the description of my book, that I had not practiced, was a less than convincing reason to write a book. I told them WHAT I was doing before WHY I was doing it.

Think of your purpose or your cause or your belief in your dream. That's what sells people on your dream, whether it's a business or adrenaline flooding activity.

If you're afraid of sharing your dreams with others, share your 'why' before revealing your goal. Connect with people on an emotional level so your goal resonates with them. If they happen to feel the same way, or perhaps you've helped them have a realization, these are the people who will support you.

Find people that share your 'why' so you can support each other in making that dream come true!

"People don't buy what you do; they buy why you do it." - Simon Sinek

7.4- What Passion Gives Your Life Meaning?

Earlier, I talked about the part of your ikigai that gives your life more meaning; it's referred to as 'what the world needs.' It is everyone's duty in this world to serve others; we are to help each other to change the world together.

When I first heard that I had a 'duty to serve others,' I was less than enthused. All I could think of was, 'What are people doing for ME?' So selfish. So naive.

After doing some research into it, I realized that it just wasn't worded properly.

'Duty to serve others' doesn't mean giving everyone free stuff, volunteering all your spare time and donating all of your money. For instance, have you ever asked for help? Or offered someone help? There's our instinctive need to help others and the 'duty to serve' is just that.

It gives your life more meaning to know you're helping someone in whatever they're doing. Saying yes to giving someone a hand means someone will give you a hand when you need it. If donating regularly isn't something you can do right now, do it when you can. Make it count.

I don't know if this counts as 'giving back', but I'm a total sucker for children selling chocolate for charity, or girl guides or cadets. It's a few dollars, you help them improve their organization and you get a tasty treat. It's win/win really.

I donate my time by visiting an elderly person at a retirement home once a week for one hour. Think about it…one hour is less than 1% of the whole week and it makes a world of difference to that person.

Another great way to donate your time, is for a local event or festival. It takes up one afternoon and you've helped a community raise money by helping out at their event. As a bonus of volunteering, you can meet a ton of new people from all different walks of life and professions. This is great way to network when improving the community is a common goal. Volunteering your time at an event related to your passion is a great way to learn and meet people that can help you in reaching your goals.

I hate to sound cliché, but it's about balance. The more good you put out into the world, the more good you get. Out of each element in ikigai, serving others is the most important, has the most impact and is the most fulfilling.

Continuously improving yourself, through skills or mindset, is key to reaching the life you've always wanted. Always work on both your mind and body. Learn new skills. Expand your mind. Your pursuit doesn't end when you reach the proverbial 'finish line.'

Did you notice as you've moved closer to your goals, more pop up? You can't expect to reach one goal and be done with it; you need to move the goal post. Dive deeper into that subject. Learn a complementary skill. Turn your skill into videos, a speech or create a course. Just don't stop moving forward. You'll never know where you could end up or what new passions you could discover!

You have to stay on top of things by improving yourself, but you also must improve your life around you; you cannot live in disarray. I talked about cycles and keeping a home free of distraction, but it's still there. You know all the crap you dumped in closets and drawers so you couldn't see it? Well, it's still distracting you, it's just out of sight. Empty a closet and reorganize, throw out and put things where they make sense. I recently emptied every drawer in my kitchen and put things where they make sense, like putting the spatulas beside the stove where they are actually used. Make your life more efficient by making things take less time. The less time you waste looking for something, or even walking across the room to get something, is time saved.

If you want more examples of making your life efficient, I recommend watching videos from Paul Akers. He is a fanatic about living his life and business lean and has a ton of videos about it. Many of them are about manufacturing, but many can be applied to your own home. Organizing your home also stops you from over-buying and continuously running out of necessities causing unnecessary stress and more distractions. Keeping things lean will help you have less clutter and more money in your pocket so you can focus on building your amazing life.

I hate to sound like a stickler, but putting everything in its place makes life a lot less complicated and way more efficient. This is where to fix what bugs you, if you can never find your keys or the cups are too far away from the fridge.

Take five minutes. Put a five-minute song on and GO GO GO. Wash as many dishes as you can or dust all the things or move one thing to a better spot. It's as easy as that, so don't tell me you don't have five minutes!

7.5 - Make Your List & Check It Twice

Just checking in…

How is your goal and dream list coming along? Make sure you look it over every few days or add to it as soon as something new you'd like to try pops into your head. The more you get into a goal mindset, the more goals you will think of! Have any stood out as something you're going to dive into right away? Are there any quick experiences that you plan on doing in the near future? Set a date and put it on social media with the hashtag #thenewbucketlist. Once you complete it, post it! I'd love to celebrate your victories with you!

Just the other day, I was watching a movie and saw something wanted to try. "I'll write it down after the movie. I'll totally remember." THAT NEVER HAPPENS. New goals are gold! Write them down immediately. I swear, every time I say I'll remember something is like hitting the delete key. Write it down as soon as possible. I keep a pad of paper and pen beside my bed because I've thought of great ideas before falling asleep and completely forget about them in the morning. The frustrating part is that I remembered that I thought of something very compelling but cannot recall what it was. Don't be that person. Write it all down, dial it in it later.

Every single day, you have a great idea or multiple great ideas that you dismiss. Get in the habit of writing them down. It doesn't matter if it's an idea for a new business or a new route to drive to work, write them down. Many songwriters say they have to get all the bad songs out of them to get to the good ones; the same thing works with ideas. Some may seem useless right now, but may become useful later.

I talked about doing a brain dump earlier in this book; this is also where you can put your ideas on paper. I like to keep my idea muscle working, so when I can't think of something specific to think of ideas for, I think of random ones. For instance, while driving, I thought of 10 other materials tires could be made of. Did my ideas make sense? No. Did it make me flex my creativity muscle? Yes. This is why not all ideas have to be brilliant, you just need to get into the habit of intentionally thinking of ideas. Once your brain is in this habit, the better the ideas become!

You need to make this practice intentional. Thinking of random ideas can also help when you're stuck. Thinking of something else can take pressure off of you if there's writer's block or you're trying to think of a way around an obstacle.

There is another way to help you focus on creating new ideas…

"You've got to write a bad song to get the good ones out!"— Lizzy Ward, Ward Thomas

7.6 - That Dopamine Tho

Don't small victories feel good? That hit of dopamine when you complete a short-term goal has great impact and becomes addictive. Pick a dream; preferably something doable on a short timeline, let's say three to six months. Make a plan. Put it on paper. Are there tasks that are big and time consuming? Break them down into smaller steps. Write down everything you'll need to do to accomplish that dream and start taking those steps.

When I booked my trip to Peru, I made a short-term goal. My goal was to order food in Spanish and I had four months to do it. Sounds doable, right?

I'd never really learned a language except the basics of French I learned from Grade 1-10. At that age, I wasn't trying nor did I know anyone that actually spoke French to learn from. Spanish was a different story; I actually WANTED to learn. So, it began!

I started waking up 15 minutes earlier every morning to do my Spanish lesson. I had downloaded an app on my phone, so it was portable, in case I slept in...accidentally. After two months, I asked a friend from Spain to go out for dinner. She helped me practice and let me know what needed work. Two months later, I was in Peru ordering my cafe con leche y zucar like a boss.

It was a specific short-term goal. I made a plan with specific steps. I executed the plan and hablo español! You can do this with any short-term goal. Long-term goals should be broken down into three- to six-month goals and those are the milestones you want to hit. Let's start making those dreams come true, shall we?

Go through your list and pick one. Plan it out. Set a date. I want you to get a taste of what your dream life can bring you. It will be amazing when you experience these small victories and you'll be craving more!

Do it!!!!

You and I are off to a good start; the list of goals is growing, you're on the lookout for your ikigai AND you've planned out how you will achieve your first goal. I'm excited!

Some goals are easy, but you don't know you can achieve them because you haven't even tried. The discomfort of trying and failing is better than the pain of never knowing. Remember that!

"You can do anything you set your mind to, but it's not going to be easy and it's not going to be fast." - Tom Bilyeu

CONCLUSION

You did it! This may be the end of our journey together, but it is just the beginning of your exciting adventure. Your list is a list in progress, to be edited and added to. Each year, choose the goals you want to tackle. I'd recommend choosing your next year's goals early, in case you need to do some preparation, like registering for a class or saving up to buy an instrument. Make your plan and give it all you've got.

The small steps make goals so much more manageable and less daunting. Sending an email isn't scary, but it's a step. Spending one hour on researching your niche instead of scrolling through Instagram isn' scary. Reading one hour of a personal development book instead o watching Netflix isn't scary. Forgoing your morning coffee or getting up a little earlier and using that extra time to meditate is probably the scaries thing for most people.

All of these little actions get you on the right track to reaching you goal. Sacrificing a little can go a long way. Once you've got momentum, i won't feel like sacrifice, it will feel empowering! It puts you in th driver's seat!

Never stop moving forward towards those goals because no one i going to do it for you. This is YOUR life. Even though not everyone i your life will be on board, you cannot use it as an excuse to give up. Th words of those people will creep up in your head when you start to ge close to creating something amazing.

Clear your mind of nagging thoughts as often as possible. Get journal or type them up to get them off your mind. Stop your monke brain from distracting you. Stop regret from creeping in to sabotage you this does not serve you.

The goal is not to expand the list of regrets you already have; the goal is to expand the list of dreams you have crossed off the list, especially the ones you'd be pissed you didn't do. Now you know you will never wonder 'What if?' You will move towards the unknown and towards discomfort. You will grow. You will thrive!

Say yes when you'd normally say no. Say yes to new experiences. It's so exciting to discover a new passion when you had said no to it before. Just because it's not on your list, doesn't mean you shouldn't try it; like Jesse Itlzer says, "Build your life resume."

To get the most out of life, take care of your mind and body. Nourish the body and clear the mind. Journaling, meditation with those fruits and veggies are all key components to creating your dream life. If you're not healthy enough to enjoy your life and be present, you're going to board the Regret Train to Sad Town. Don't let your 90-year-old self down!

Your 90-year-old self would be pissed that you allowed yourself to get taken advantage of and wasted precious time, so break the cycle now. Say no. Use the time you're saving from doing things you don't want to do and work on your dreams. Cut out toxic people. Accept the Bubble People as they are. Find a like-minded friend to help encourage you, and where you can, encourage others. You will never hear from a hater doing better than you; remember that when the Bubble People/doubters/downers and people afraid to go after their dreams creep up. You are simply reminding the Bubble People that they are in the same spot they've always been.

Be vulnerable. Connect with people. Tell others, especially the Bubble People, what your dream means to you and how you would feel achieving it. Sharing those emotions with others encourages them to share theirs as well. It's the best way to form new relationships and friendships, and gives you the opportunity to meet even more amazing people. You never know when you will meet the person you need that can propel you towards your goal and you never know, you might be that person for someone else!

You may not be able to find others take this journey with you right away; they may find you! Accept the help you are offered. This is a sign;

being offered the help that you need is a gift from the universe that you are going in the right direction. There are many people out there just like us, compelled to serve others and to live their life to the fullest. Remember that serving others is another aspect of feeling fulfilled, that's why others will offer you help, and you should do the same.

Our old friend fear, an old identity, is one of those toxic friends you need to leave behind. I'm not just talking about the fear of success, I'm talking about a lifelong crippling fear, that fear everyone close to you knows about and makes arrangements around. This is your time to let go. This is your time to put in the work to stop fear in its tracks and open up a whole new part of your life you had never experienced before. From crying in a swimming pool in front of strangers, I can tell you, it won't be easy, but it WILL be worth it.

Keep your head up. Let that pronoia thrive and reframe the negatives into learning experiences. Break the cycle of self-sabotage and accept that you deserve your dream life. Visualize that dream life every single day as you move towards it. Daily, I want you to look over your plan for the first goal you're going to tackle. You got this!

You are fighting the clock and you don't even know when it ends. We are all in the same fight...some stay in the game longer than others. It's shitty to think about, but it's reality, so make the most of it. I never thought I'd lose a friend so young and I'm sure he had no idea his life would be cut short so soon. He probably had plans and goals that he thought he had time to do.

It took a tragedy to get me to this stage. It was horrible to lose someone I cared about who helped me out of my own misery, but I know I'd be living an unfulfilled life without this wakeup call. One would normally blame a tragedy for all that is bad in their lives, but that means one would also need to blame that same tragedy for all good that happens in light of it. I'm not saying Chris' death was a good thing, but if something negative happens in life, the best thing one can do is learn from it and take action.

I lost a great friend, confidant and cheerleader, but I gained a whole new perspective that turned my life upside down for the better.

Really think about how you view death and how you will use Mortality Motivation to push you forward towards all of those goals. Think about how your new insight will change how you prioritize and make time. Which goals would you be pissed you didn't get to do if you died today? Which goal will take the longest? What's the first step towards just one of those goals?

Your list of dreams and goals is ongoing. I want you to always add to it as you cross things off the list. Have a journal or notepad with you to write down your amazing ideas. As I learned, not all ideas seem good at the time, but there is a time and a place for all of them. Don't forget to post your adventures using the hashtag #thenewbucketlist! I can't wait to see what you do, and I'll be cheering you on!

I've said it 100 times, but I will say it again...the bane of human existence is that there is an expiry date on each and every person. Let this ticking clock help you say yes when you'd normally say no, be open to trying new things and keeping your eye on the prize, your dream life.

Take what we've learned from this and live your life...and I mean REALLY live it! I hate to sound cliché, but you only live once.

ABOUT THE AUTHOR

If you've gotten this far, you know that Lisa is hilarious…or at least she *thinks* she's hilarious.

She's been thinking outside of the box and asking, "WHY NOT?!" her whole life. It's not a surprise she wrote this book about getting out of your comfort zone since she's always been pushing those around her to try anything and everything. Lisa loves to cheer people on when they have their sights on goals and to celebrate everyone's success.

Lisa was born in Oshawa, Ontario, but now resides in Toronto. She has a huge family, mostly residing in Ontario, but also has family in Western Canada and the Netherlands. She is a food lover, beer lover, animal lover and will probably ask to pet your dog.

Lisa is an avid reader and exercise enthusiast. She practices what she preaches and has motivational sayings, her perfect day, goals and what she's grateful for decorating her condo. She calls herself an extroverted introvert, where she loves to talk to and meet people, but also loves alone time to reflect and relax.

Don't forget to follow her adventures on Instagram @livethenewbucketlist and www.thenewbucketlist.com. Hashtag when you get out of your comfort zone #livethenewbucketlist so she can feature you and inspire others!

YOU GOT THIS

Printed in Great Britain
by Amazon

43234135R00066